is THERE ONLY ONE

CHICAGO

by KENAN HEISE

D1568044

Westover
Publishing Company

A Media General Publication, Richmond, Virginia

SBN 0-87858-034-4

Contents

PREFACE

Chicago is no island. It's right in the middle of everything that's American — for better and for worse.

The railroads and airlines converge here. And the people convene in this city to promote their professions, their political parties, their businesses, their causes. It's the town Americans visit at least twice.

This book about Chicago has been put together to satisfy the curiosity of New Yorkers, Iowans, Californians and above all, Chicagoans.

All questions and answers in these pages first appeared in Action Line, a newspaper column that is itself a Chicago institution. The author has been editor of it since 1965.

Action Line began that year in Chicago's American and has continued in its successor, Chicago Today. Readers send in questions, complaints and problems — more than one million so far. The column has tried to solve or answer all of them.

Delightfully, Chicagoans in the midst of seeking lost relatives or looking for a way out of a tangle of red tape, have demonstrated an all-encompassing curiosity about their city.

Why are there two right angle curves in Lake Shore Drive? Where is Al Capone buried? How many Frank Lloyd Wright buildings are there in Chicago?

Some of the older Chicagoans wanted to check their memories: Did a blimp once fall through the roof of a LaSalle Street bank? How valuable were the spittoons in the Everleigh sisters' world-famous bordello? And what ever happened to the old Green Hornet streetcars?

People had questions about Chicago's political history: Wasn't there a mayor of Chicago elected on the Know-Nothing ticket? Why did Mayor Big Bill Thompson set out for the South Seas looking for tree-climbing fish?

Chicago is not always sensible, but it is sometimes sensitive and it wanted to know about people like Jane Addams, Mother Cabrini, Frank Lloyd Wright, sculptor Lorado Taft and the tragic boxer, Jack Johnson.

The research has been exhilarating, whether it involved finding a participant in Houdini's famous debunking of a Chicago medium or locating the gallows stored in the boiler room of the Criminal Courts Building for Terrible Tommy O'Connor, who escaped four days before he was to hang in 1921.

The "we" who dug for the facts included a wonderful group of more than 20 people who served at one time or other on the staff of Action Line. Among those who helped do the writing have been Chuck McWhinnie, Milton Hansen and Bernie Hanley.

Much of the research was done in old newspaper clippings and it was never easy to get the complete story. And that's a must when you're writing about incidents in which a few or many of your readers may have participated.

The answers you read in these pages have stood the test of more than 700,000 readers having the opportunity to challenge them. We're proud of their accuracy.

Others who have contributed have included the library (morgue) staff of Chicago Today, especially Al Wykel and Augie Jewell. They often checked a 5th or 6th and sometimes a 56th reference to help us get a complete answer. This kind of cooperation we also received from the Chicago Public Library and the Chicago Tribune library.

I also want to say "thank you" — simply and directly — to the editors of Chicago Today, especially Lloyd Wendt, for encouraging both Action Line and the publication of this book. The pictures used here are reprinted with their permission and through their kindness.

Above all, I want to acknowledge all Chicagoans, from the Indian who first named a smelly creek "Chicagou" to Mayor Daley, who manages (or does he?) to look so much like the Picasso sculpture in the Civic Center Plaza.

Kenan Heise

INTRODUCTION

The title of this delightful hit-and-run look at the Second City might have been "Everything You Always Wanted to Know About Chicago and Weren't Afraid to Ask." Because the book is, in reality, a collaboration between curious residents of Chicago and suburbs with questions on their minds, and Kenan Heise and the tireless staff of Chicago Today's Action Line, who put the answers together.

I suppose it is nonsense to say this, but I am firmly and irretrievably convinced that there is NO query relating to Chicago for which Kenan Heise or one of his fellow ransackers couldn't find an answer. They are like squirrels who know where every nut is buried, and if that seems a rude analogy, they are like librarians who are familiar with the contents, or at least the potential, of every volume in some vast reference collection.

It would demand someone like Kenan (or his counterpart on The Tribune's Action Express, Dave Thompson) to head up a project such as Action Line. Kenan, who in his early years studied for the priesthood, is one of the most concerned men I've ever met. He seems to thrive on solving problems for people — which is basically what Action Line is all about.

And when you get a bright-type guy, who can't stand not knowing about something, and who worries about coming up with the perfect response to problems or questions large or small, and put him in Kenan's situation, success is assured. I asked him, in fact, whether there had been queries he and his associates had failed to satisfy. He admitted, unhappily, that there had been a few. These were the exceptions, as a quick run-through of the following pages will prove.

Whether the seeker-of-information wishes to know where she can have the family Chevrolet squashed flat enough and compactly enough to serve as a coffee-table (cross my heart), or whether it is true that a burning blimp once crashed thru the roof of a bank building in the Loop, killing a number of persons, Action Line is ready, willing, and eager to oblige.

The result of seven years of serving as a kind of corporate ombudsman for the readers of Chicago Today has been a mass of perceptive or oddball or flippant questions which, together with a bunch of perceptive or oddball or flippant answers, make a patchwork picture of Chicago that tells a great deal more about the town than does many a more pretentious work.

This is a book that is ideal for browsing through — whether your interests center on architecture, history, ghosts, catastrophes, gangsters, politics or any of a variety of topics. It also is a book for the settlement of arguments, for laughing at, or weeping over, for the skeptic or for the chauvinist. It has, in a word, something for everyone.

It is, in addition, an ideal gift for Doubting Thomases from San Francisco or Keokuk or London or Bombay who don't believe all they've heard about the town that over a century or so has played host to Louis Sullivan, Mary Garden, Al Capone, Lorado Taft, Clarence Darrow, Steve Allen, Ernie Banks, Big Bill Thompson, Red Grange, Bill Veeck, Gwendolyn Brooks, Hugh Hefner, the McCormick family, the Great Chicago Fire, the Black Sox, the Stockyards, Oak Street Beach, the Hancock Building (which during construction was described, with a kind of inverse snobbery, as intended to be "18 feet shorter than the Empire State"), and too many other unique individuals or things to set down.

It is a primer for the newcomer to Chicago history, a refresher course for those who have forgotten, a reference work for budding historians, and a dandy way to pass the time for anyone with an inquisitive kind of mind.

I personally miss the presence of some of the more personal kinds of problem-solving for which Action Line is justly famous. The righting of wrongs or errors, the placing of lamps along shadowy corridors, the proof that if you are a little guy it pays to know a big guy if you have a justifiable beef about something.

But as Kenan says, that's a different book altogether and would only diffuse the focus of this one, which portrays Chicago, in text and photograph, from a variety of vantage points and in a number of aspects which may surprise even the most knowledgeable of Chicago buffs leafing through its pages. And I refuse to argue with anyone who, as I've said, already knows the answers.

Robert Cromie
Chicago, Illinois

Only
One
Chicago

*"Is there only one
Chicago?"*
—Geri Muskus

In the United States, in the whole world, there is only one. The cartographic division of Rand McNally & Co. says that once upon a time there was a post office in Missouri with the name Chicago. It no longer exists. There are a number of variations of Chicago such as Chicago Heights, New Chicago in Indiana, and Nuevo Chicago, a section of Buenos Aires. We can't imagine why other people wouldn't want to name their town after an old Indian word meaning "onion creek."

*"Who was the guy on radio who used to say, 'It's a beautiful day in Chicago'? He would say it, as I remember, every day, no matter how bleak the weather or news. I've asked a number of people and everybody remembers the expression, but not the man's name."—
K. L., Downers Grove*

For 35 years — from 1932 to 1967 — Chicago heard that phrase every day (except the day of the great blizzard of 1967) from Everett Mitchell, host of WMAQ's National Farm and Home Hour. Back in the Depression, Mitchell got tired of everyone singing the blues, especially three men he listened to one morning on his suburban train. When he got outside the train station, he explained, "I looked up at the sky. There's an old saying that if there's enough blue in the sky to mend a Dutchman's pants, it's going to be a beautiful day. So there was that patch of blue and I said to myself, 'It's a beautiful day.'" He opened his program that day with the line. During World War II when GIs on Italy's Anzio Beach were sloshing hip-deep in mud, one got a rise out of the rest of the line, "But don't forget, it's still a beautiful day in Chicago."

"This has been nagging me every day while driving to work. Why did Chicago put two right angle turns in Lake Shore Drive just south of the Chicago River?"—R.H.

Two reasons: To keep the cost of constructing the bridge there down to $2 million and to avoid years of delay in condemning warehouse property. The decision, however, turned out to be a real bummer. Construction of the bridge started in 1931 during the Depression and was delayed from 1932 to 1937 because the city ran out of money. When finally completed, the structure's cost had spiraled from $2 million to $11,575,000. Another factor involved was the future. Planners had hoped, with the aid of federal money, to use the east-west portion as an extension of Wacker Drive, building a roadway linking Michigan Avenue and Lake Shore Drive. The north-south section would be extended southward. The funds never were available, but the Chicago Department of Streets and Sanitation has plans to make these improvements "within the next three to six years," fulfilling a dormant dream.

"Could you tell me where Al Capone is buried?"—Ricky Bowbal

Chicago's most infamous gangster lies in an inconspicuous grave in Mount. Carmel Cemetery, Hillside. A simple headstone marked his resting place in a family plot until it was stolen in 1972. A gray stone cross about four feet high and bearing the family name several feet away is the only other indication of the grave of "Scarface Al." Now, he lies in an unmarked grave. However, Capone was not originally buried in Mount Carmel. On Feb. 5, 1947, Capone's coffin, topped by a blanket of gardenias and 50 orchids, was lowered into a grave in Mount Olivet Cemetery at 111th Street and California Avenue. The body later was transferred to Mount Carmel. The 48-year-old gangster died in his $100,000 retirement villa near Miami Beach on Jan. 25, 1947. A stroke followed by an attack of pneumonia killed Capone, who had suffered 9 years from advanced syphilis.

"We have heard that Mother Cabrini, who founded Columbus Hospital here, is buried in New York. My sister says she died there, but I am sure that she died right here in Chicago. Can you set us straight?"—Maria Garafolo

Mother Cabrini, that veritable dynamo of charity and administrative skill, died in Columbus Hospital here in Chicago on Dec. 22, 1917. She was later to become the first American saint of the Catholic Church. Before her death, she virtually whizzed over North, Central, and South America, founding orphanages, schools, hospitals, and convents. In Brazil, and later in Rome, she nearly died of malaria, but she kept going to finish the work on Columbus Hospital in Seattle. She was buried in New York.

"What do the letters ORD on the baggage tags at O'Hare International Airport stand for? We had a long discussion in a bar last night and nobody knew."—John Bivens, Rosemont

If we were to publish a list of the top 10 "Do you really know your Chicago?" questions, yours would make it. The ORD is short for Orchard Place Airport, the name O'Hare had during World War II when it was merely a runway to accommodate the four-engine Skymaster transports which Douglas Aircraft Company was building in a war plant there. The ORD, an O'Hare spokesman said, was kept although the name was changed to Chicago O'Hare International Airport in 1949, because the FAA is "very reluctant to change call letters." Idlewild's letters were made JFK, however, after the New York airport was renamed in honor of the late President.

"How many buildings designed by Frank Lloyd Wright are still standing in Chicago? As an art student, I would also like to know where I could find additional information on Wright and his architecture."
—Peggy Pulick

Wright experts tell us there are 14 of his buildings still standing in the city, in addition to the interior court of the Rookery Building, 209 S. LaSalle St., which he also designed. The building itself was designed by another noted architect, John W. Root. There are approximately 60 of Wright's buildings in the Chicago area, many of them in Oak Park and River Forest. The Art Institute publishes a pamphlet on the location and history of Wright's structures, as does the Oak Park Public Library.

"My sister and I are sort of chubby, so we do exercises together. To music, yet. The other day, my grandfather, who is a very dapper fellow, walked in and saw us huffing and puffing. He said, 'Ha! Just like the Beef Trust.' When we asked him what that is, or was, he simply smiled. After talking it over, we thought we'd better ask you for the answer."
—Ginny and Pam

Your grandfather must be a dapper fellow indeed, with a sense of humor, yet. The Beef Trust he was referring to was a creation of the 1930s, when novelty acts were added to vaudeville and burlesque bills to increase attendance. It was simply a group of very fat girl dancers — a sort of overstuffed version of the Playboy bunny. The famous Beef Trust in Chicago was at the old Rialto Theater, where the girls were billed as 'all under 21 and over 200 pounds.' Once, as a promotion stunt, eight of the girls (2,000 pounds worth) leaped aboard the last hansom cab in Chicago. The horse suffered a fatal heart attack trying to pull them away, and the cab collapsed into splinters moments later. Today, thanks to low-calorie foods, they don't hardly build 'em like that no more.

Characters
and Other
Famous
Chicagoans

"Could you help me settle a discussion with my children. We recently went down to Chinatown at Cermak Road and Wentworth Avenue. I happened to mention to the kids that I remember when Cermak was mayor of Chicago, but not when Wentworth was, since he was the city's first mayor. The kids claimed I was wrong, and that it was not Wentworth. My memory tells me he was the first. Who's right?"—N. Appel

Your kids. Long John Wentworth was the editor of the first Chicago newspaper and later served as mayor for two terms, 1857 and 1860. He was a flamboyant mayor in the Big Bill Thompson style and once introduced the Prince of Wales, later King Edward VII, to citizens from a hotel balcony by saying, "Boys, this is the Prince of Wales. Prince, these are the boys." Standing 6 feet, 6 inches tall, he enjoyed making vice and gambling raids. He once set one up by luring all the men in a tough area to a dog fight elsewhere. The good citizens then invaded the district, tearing down shanties, burning dens of iniquity and looting the area. The gamblers, thieves and prostitutes retaliated by setting up neighborhoods. (See p. 32 for first mayor of Chicago.)

"I have a couple of questions about Jane Addams, who founded Hull House. Did she establish the first settlement house ever? Also, could you find out whether she ever worked for the city?"—R. Mann

No, Jane Addams didn't found the first settlement house, although her Hull House became the model for those to follow. She had visited one in London; another had been in existence in New York. Our times, however, have not caught up with the visions Jane Addams had in the 1890s as Hull House nurtured a day care center, adult education, incipient labor organizing (the Amalgamated Clothing Workers of America was born there), the civil rights movement (Jane Addams was a founder of the NAACP) and the peace movement, which helped her win the 1931 Nobel Peace Prize. In 1892, she held her only job with the city — garbage inspector of the 19th Ward. Among other accomplishments, she managed to find pavement under eight inches of garbage on one narrow street. She rode herd over garbage collectors and escorted careless landlords into court until the alderman introduced and got passed an ordinance making her job a civil service one under the ward supervisor. She had to return to other pursuits.

"Some of us old-timers who live in the Hilliard Center housing project at Cermak Road and State Street like to sit around in the evening and talk about the old days. Those of us who were in Chicago around the turn of the century remember that where we now live then was called 'The Levee' and it was one of the most notorious red-light districts in the country. Could you tell us where to find out more about the area?"—One Who Remembers

You live on the southern border of what once was 'The Levee,' the sordid domain controlled by those colorful villians of Chicago politics, Bathhouse John Coughlin and Hinky Dink Kenna. Right on your doorstep, at 2131-33 S. Dearborn St., was the most famous bordello of them all — the Everleigh Club. It was a 50-room mansion which sported a $15,000 gold piano, rare books, costly statuary, oil paintings, gold silk curtains, gilded bathtubs, and 20 gold-plated spittoons. Ada and Minna, the sisters who ran the club, closed shop in 1911. A history of the area is contained in the book "Lords of The Levee" by Lloyd Wendt and Herman Kogan, which is available at the public library.

SOUTH SIDE LEVEE
in 1910

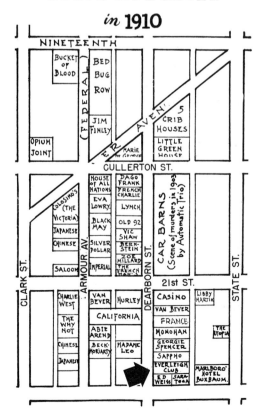

"You told about the Everleigh Sisters, Chicago's most famous madams. What I would like to know is whether they were both all that attractive?"—A Curious Woman

As business women, they were excelled by none. As beauty queens, they should be judged by their pictures, which we are printing for your benefit.

"A radio personality objected to the item in the Action Line about the gold piano in the Everleigh Club. He said that no house of that sort would bother furnishing the place with an expensive piano. Who's right?"—S.R.

Obviously, the disk jockey is not an expert on turn-of-the-century houses of ill repute. We checked the sources that are. The book, "Lords of The Levee" by Kogan and Wendt gave a $15,000 value to that piano. Charles Washburn, who wrote "Come Into My Parlor," a book about the Everleigh Sisters, bought the piano after the Everleigh Club closed down. He said the gold leaf alone cost $2,000. The gold-plated spittoons, by the way, reportedly cost $650 each.

"Has anyone ever written a book about Paddy Bauler? We used to enjoy reading about him in the papers."—A Curious Husband and Wife

Nobody's confined Paddy between the covers of a book yet, and it's too bad. Paddy started off as a garbage truck driver and rose to fame as Chicago's 43d Ward alderman, retiring after 30 years in 1967. His most famous comment was: "Chicago ain't ready for reform." Paddy gained additional fame as a fantastic world traveler. He'd take off for Tokyo, Vienna or Hong Kong as though he were taking the El to the Loop. Munich had always been a favorite destination because he liked that city's beer. Paddy's Chicago-style politics were front and center the time Mayor Edward J. Kelly relayed a garbage complaint from one of Bauler's Gold Coast residents. Paddy asked the mayor if he knew how many votes he had gotten in that precinct. The mayor said he didn't. Paddy answered: "I got one. Let the lady pick up her own garbage."

Prominent Chicagoan Clarence Darrow lost many cases, even some of his most famous ones. He did have many triumphs and a number of his defeats turned to victory. The Chicago lawyer never lost a defendant to the death penalty, saving 220 including men convicted of such crimes as shooting a policeman and dynamiting a newspaper office, killing 21 persons. He saved thrill-killers Leopold and Loeb from the electric chair. Darrow was a "gentle pessimist," seeing the best in the worst and the worst in the best of men (including Clarence Darrow). He once said of himself, "I've never killed anyone, but I frequently get satisfaction out of reading the obituary."

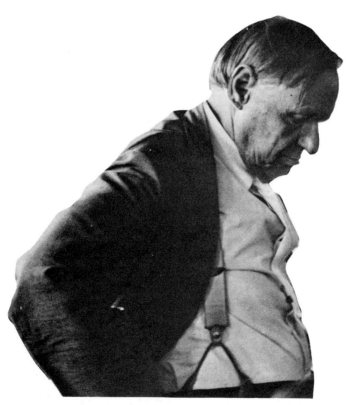

"Could you tell me about Al Capone? I have just recently come here from Japan, and my friends and I are very curious about this infamous man. I have visited his grave site, but I would like to learn more."—Toshiaki

Retired Chicago Today writer George Murray, whose books have dealt with the Capone crime syndicate, wrote the following capsule biography of "Scarface Al" for you. He was born in 1899 at Castellamare, a little town south of Naples. Capone came to Chicago in 1922 from Brooklyn. (Some sources say he was born there.) He first attracted police attention when arrested for drawing a pistol on a cab driver. The name he gave was Antonio Caponi, and he said he was living at the old Four Deuces brothel at 2222 Wabash Ave. By means of violence and terror, Capone quickly gained control of every organized illicit activity in the city and neighboring suburbs. In 1927, Capone reportedly made 105 million dollars — the highest gross individual income ever recorded. Even Henry Ford could claim only 70 million dollars during his peak years. After his conviction for evading income taxes, Capone left Chicago on May, 1932, to enter Atlanta penitentiary. He died Jan. 25, 1947.

"Please tell the truth about Amos 'n' Andy. I claim that back when they were at the height of their popularity, movie houses would stop their performances whenever the program would come on. My wife simply cannot believe this, so I'm depending on you to set her straight."
—D.S.M.

In the 1930s, whenever Amos 'n' Andy came on the air, America came to a screeching halt. According to newspaper clippings of the day, everybody listened. Movie houses, whose attendance dropped to nil on Amos 'n' Andy night, wooed their patrons back by promises of an intermission with the radio program piped in. Lovers would stop smooching, arguments would cease and some bartenders even refused to serve when the Mystic Knights of the Sea Lodge took to the airways. From the time Freeman (Amos) Gosden and Charles (Andy) Correll made their first broadcast on March 19, 1928, they were an instant, resounding success. Forced off the air by a growing sensitivity on the subject of race relations, Amos 'n' Andy became the victims of reform — something they always did their level best to avoid.

"For years, Dad kept hanging on to some worthless Insull Utility Investment certificates. He always told me that someday he'd tell me about Samuel Insull. Dad never had the opportunity, however, and he recently died. Anything you can tell me about Insull might help me figure out what my father had on his chest."—C.J.

If there is a moral in the Sam Insull tale, it would have to be stressing caution. Insull came to this country from London in the late 1800s. By 1907, he rose from Thomas A. Edison's private secretary to the leadership of a utilities empire in Chicago. When the 1930s were ushered in, Insull's personal fortune was estimated at $150 million. During the early Depression days, the tycoon felt he could do no wrong. When his stocks started to slip, he tried to hold their prices by using money borrowed from eastern banks to buy shares in his own companies. When his creditors pulled the rug from under him, Insull couldn't believe it. And neither could a million investors when the crash came. Insull later faced mail fraud charges and was acquitted. He died virtually penniless in 1938.

"I used to live in an area bounded by Milwaukee, North, and Damen Avenues. During the 1930s, there was a guy who was flagpole-sitting around here. Can you verify this?"—Terry Grace

Flagpole squatters were far too numerous to cover in those days. The most famous we could pinpoint was a Joe (Flagpole) Powers, a chap who had an uncontrollable desire to shinny up rods. He once sat on a pole atop a building at 2800 Milwaukee Avenue in August of 1930, with the hope of eclipsing Shipwreck Kelly's record of staying aloft for 50 days in Atlantic City, N.J. Joe never made it, and Perry Will's mark on Jan. 2, 1960, relegated both men to obscurity anyway when the Terre Haute, Ind., truckdriver sat for 232 days. Flagpole Joe, though, gained his notoriety by perching atop the Morrison Hotel's pole for 17 days in July of 1927. A violent storm thrashed him around while up there and he lost a couple of teeth. Two dentists fixed him up with new choppers, aided by an impression taken some 600 feet in the air. Joe secretly scurried up the hotel's pole again in 1934, but Morrison people called the police, who coaxed him down and did some head scratching in order to come up with a charge.

"My U.S. history class was recently discussing treason and we got on the subject of Tokyo Rose. Could you find out what happened to her since she was convicted of treason? Approximately how old was she when she made her radio broadcasts?"—Kathy Briarton

Mrs. Iva Ikuko Toguri D'Aquino was in the news again recently when the government subpoenaed her financial records in an attempt to collect the balance of a $10,000 fine levied as part of her treason conviction. A graduate of U.C.L.A., Tokyo Rose served 6 1/2 years of a 10-year sentence. After she was released in 1956, she lived in Chicago, protecting her anonymity. Rose was convicted in 1949 of just one of the eight charges of treason against her, the "so-called statement concerning ships," of which there was no record, tape or transcript. She allegedly said, "Now that you have lost all your ships you really are orphans of the Pacific. How do you think you will ever get home?" The foreman of the jury apologized to her for the verdict. She was born in 1916.

Oscar F. Mayer, the last of the meat packing titans, died on March 11, 1955, less than three weeks before his 96th birthday. Born in Germany on March 29, 1859, Mayer came to America in 1873, and at 24 started his dynasty with an investment of $2,000. Mayer remained active in his business for 72 years. One old clipping claimed he preferred fish and poultry over meat. Mayer also once said, "When you retire, you grow old," and made daily visits to the plant until four weeks before he died. The firm vigorously denies his preference for chicken and fish.

33

"*How many votes did Brian Flanagan get for sheriff of Cook County in 1970? We have a bet whether or not it was enough to influence the results.*"—Jake

Brian Flanagan, the Weatherman who tangled with Richard Elrod, who was elected sheriff, received more campaign publicity than he did votes. According to the official canvass, he got 27 votes. Elrod received 887,028 votes and Republican Bernard Carey, 876,549. Daffy Duck got his usual one vote.

History

"When I was a kid, just before World War II, my father took me to see a replica of Fort Dearborn. It was someplace near the lake, but I don't remember exactly where. Could you tell me when it was built, where it was, and what became of it?"—
John Carlson

You were in the "third Fort Dearborn," which was built for A Century of Progress Exposition in 1933. The building stood at 26th Street and the lake. It was virtually abandoned after the fair closed its doors and, despite the efforts of civic groups to save it, finally succumbed to vandalism and fire in the early war years. The original fort — on the south bank of the Chicago River at Michigan Avenue — was burned after the massacre in 1812, but was reconstructed in 1816. It stood until 1867, when it was heavily damaged by fire. Parts of the fort were saved and can be seen at the Chicago Historical Society.

FT. DEARBORN, FROM THE WEST, 1808.

"Can you help me with any information about a cemetery which was in Lincoln Park off North Avenue at Clark Street?

I remember people talking about it and told a friend. He says there never was such a place."—Roland Reher, Cary

There was. From 1837 to 1865, the south end of Lincoln Park was the original Rosehill Cemetery. Then the graves were moved and the area was made into a park. Two pioneers buried there, however, remained as a memorial after the rest of the bodies were moved. Ira Couch, who, along with his brother, built Tremont House, an early Chicago hotel, is buried in the mausoleum. The last surviving member of the Boston Tea Party, David Kennison, has his grave marked by a boulder off Clark Street at about 1900 north.

Could you tell me how many bridges there are in Chicago that go up and down or swing sideways? Also could you give me a little history of such bridges?"—
Archie Ames

Chicago has 55 movable bridges spanning the Chicago and Calumet Rivers. Their operation costs 2.3 million dollars a year and that involves 33,000 openings and closings. The first one was stationary — built in 1831 at Wolf Point (just west of where the Merchandise Mart is). The Pottawatomie Indians and the settlers each put up about $250 to build it. It didn't last long, though, because the settlers carried it off, log by log, for firewood over the long, hard winter. If you're looking for a job as a bridgetender and don't have any political connections, forget it. The last civil service examination for the job was given in 1953.

William B. Ogden, a Democrat, was elected to the $500-a-year office in 1837, a time when 709 eligible voters out of the 4,170 total population showed up to vote. Sworn in at Russell's saloon, the real estate wizard played an important role during Chicago's embryonic stages. Naming one of those confusing criss-cross streets after the man may seem like a small tribute. Ogden built the first drawbridge over the Chicago River, laid out miles of streets and roads, promoted the Illinois and Michigan Canal, and did a great deal to develop the parks, sewage and water supply systems of Chicago. He was president of the board of trustees of the first "University of Chicago," helped build the first McCormick reaper plant and supported the Theological Seminary of the Northwest, the Academy of Sciences and the Astronomical Society. His "absolute faith in Chicago" (projects financed at his own expense) once brought him $3 million for some land that eight years before cost him $8,000.

"When I ride the train every morning, I really admire those old homes which were built by the Pullman Car Company around 105th and Cottage Grove Avenue. I've heard that they are as sturdy and as sound as a gold piece, and the people who have them sure keep them in good condition. Could you give me some of their history?"—D.A.F.

George M. Pullman needed an immense plant for his Pullman Palace Car Company, and he wanted a "model industrial town" to go along with it. Nearly 3,500 acres were purchased on the western shore of Lake Calumet, which was then outside the city limits of Chicago. The plant and town together cost 8 million dollars to build back in 1881. Today, all but two buildings of the plant are gone, but the red-brick town remains, a monument to city planning of yesteryear. Originally, the project was a veritable garden, with flowers everywhere. A modern touch was its own shopping center. To the workers though, it was just the "company store" where they bought everything else, from Pullman. The residents grew tired of the arrangement, and annexed themselves to Chicago in 1889. After the great strike of 1894, the property was sold to individuals. Pullman, by the way, said the town was named both for him and S.S. Beman, its architect. The first syllable of his name was used along with the last syllable of Beman, he jested.

"You seem to like questions about the history of Chicago. Here's one: What national convention held here met in a wigwam?"—R. Rudders

You make them easy. It was the Republican convention of May 16, 1860, at which Lincoln was nominated for the Presidency. The "wigwam" was the wooden convention hall specially built for the event at Lake and Market (now Wacker Drive) Streets. The building was constructed in such haste that cynical Chicagoans dubbed it "The Wigwam," which was current slang for any lean-to or flimsily built shed. The name stuck, to the dismay of those politicos who had money in the project. Convention halls lead ill-starred lives in the Windy City, and the wigwam burned in the great fire of 1871.

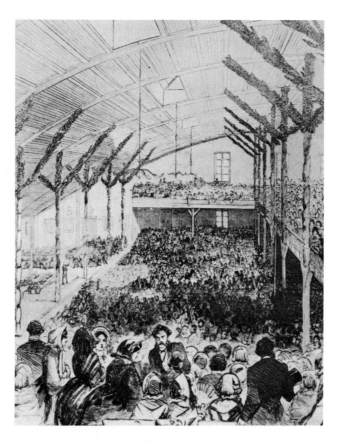

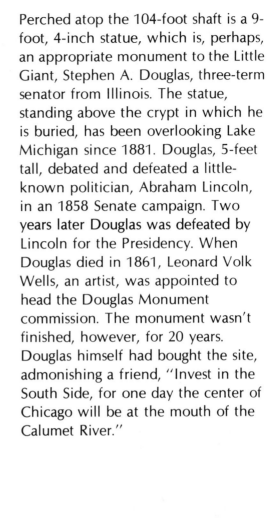

"There is a monument somewhere around 35th Street that can be seen from Lake Shore Drive. I would like to know more about it. I used to pass it every day but never had a chance to take a closer look."—Debbie Roberts

Perched atop the 104-foot shaft is a 9-foot, 4-inch statue, which is, perhaps, an appropriate monument to the Little Giant, Stephen A. Douglas, three-term senator from Illinois. The statue, standing above the crypt in which he is buried, has been overlooking Lake Michigan since 1881. Douglas, 5-feet tall, debated and defeated a little-known politician, Abraham Lincoln, in an 1858 Senate campaign. Two years later Douglas was defeated by Lincoln for the Presidency. When Douglas died in 1861, Leonard Volk Wells, an artist, was appointed to head the Douglas Monument commission. The monument wasn't finished, however, for 20 years. Douglas himself had bought the site, admonishing a friend, "Invest in the South Side, for one day the center of Chicago will be at the mouth of the Calumet River."

"My grandfather told me when I was young that the lake used to come up to Michigan Avenue, and the Illinois Central tracks were actually out in the lake. I've looked through old pictures of the city, and can't find any evidence of it. I should think the lake waves would have washed trains right off the tracks if it were true."—Sarah Gaines

Grandpa was right, but he was living "way back when" to remember it. The Illinois Central built tracks on a trestle in the lake back in 1853. The city ordinance allowing it required them to put in a breakwater to protect both the tracks and the waterfront. The lagoon inside the tracks lasted until the fire of 1871, when it was used to dump "tens of thousands of wagon-loads of ashes, debris, stone fragments, melted nails and spikes, and slag from the city's ruins." The body of water was completely filled in and the railroad tracks were on terra firma from then on.

"Could you please find out something for us about the Civil War prisoner of war camp that was here in Chicago? How bad was it and where was it?"—Jane Oesterreich

Camp Douglas was near the lake, just south of the city limits, between what is now 31st and 35th Streets. The land originally belonged to Sen. Stephen A. Douglas, the man Abraham Lincoln defeated for the Presidency in 1860. In 1861, it served as a mustering center for Union troops recruited in the surrounding area. In February, 1862, 7,000 Confederate prisoners were stockaded there. All things considered, they were treated rather humanely and Chicagoans raised more than $100,000 for the prisoners' benefit. They were fed 14 ounces of beef or 10 ounces of pork and 14 ounces of bread a day, a meat diet that is not matched in our local jails today. Overcrowding, the cold weather and the wounds of war, however, did eventually take their toll and several thousand died in the last three years of the war. A plot to release the prisoners and to capture Chicago in the name of the Confederacy was foiled on the day Lincoln was reelected in 1864.

"What is the location of Mrs. O'Leary's barn where the cow kicked over the lantern"
—*Mrs. L.K.*

Mrs. O'Leary's house and barn were at what is now the Chicago Fire Academy, 558 De Koven St. The fire started Sunday evening, Oct. 8, 1871. Three cows and a horse occupied Mrs. O'Leary's barn when the fire broke out. Though the legend blames one of the cows, the origin of the great fire which killed 250 and left 100,000 homeless was never determined.

"Can you get me some information on the Chicago fire? I tried writing a few places but didn't get one reply."—
Gayle Christopher

By Sunday evening, Oct. 8, 1871, all the prerequisites for a holocaust were present in Chicago. The total rainfall for the summer was only 2 1/2 inches instead of the normal 9 inches. Of the city's 60,000 buildings, about 40,000 were constructed entirely of wood and the city council was apathetic to the fire marshal's request to install larger water mains. Although legend blames one of Mrs. O'Leary's cows, the inferno's origin was never really determined. Amazingly, only 250 to 300 persons died in the fire that laid waste to 2,200 acres, destroyed 15,768 buildings, left 94,000 homeless, and cost Chicago an estimated 188 million dollars. The Chicago Public Library's history and travel department has information and will help you ferret it out if you'll drop in. The Chicago Historical Society, Clark Street and North Avenue, has pictures and brochures available.

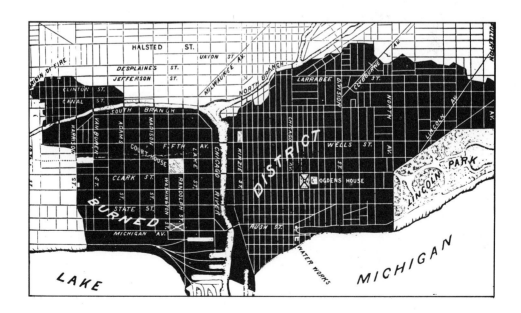

"Recently, I was reading some family diaries that told about seeing the Chicago Fire all the way up in Lake Geneva, Wis. With the recent centennial of the fire I wondered how far away the fire could be seen. Could you find out?"
—*Gloria Van Dyke, Mount Prospect*

According to Herman Kogan, who with Bob Cromie wrote the book, "The Great Fire: Chicago 1871," it could easily have been viewed in the sky from Lake Geneva. While no records of the distance from which the conflagration could be seen can be found, the fire was reportedly "felt" up to 800 miles away, off Cape Hatteras, N.C., where a ship was inundated with ashes the wind had swept aloft. It was said the fire was so bright in Des Plaines, 20 miles away, a person could read a newspaper by it. Workmen in Holland, Mich., were reported to have sought shelter from scorching winds that crossed the lake.

"Can you tell me what the oldest company in Chicago is? I'm curious to know whether any present day company goes back before the Chicago Fire of 1871."
—Terry Tivnan

The oldest company in Chicago is C.D. Peacock Co., jewelers, at State and Monroe Streets. The firm was founded in 1837 by Elijah Peacock, who came from England as a clockmaker and repairman of ships' chronometers. The company still has some of Elijah's old records, as well as his diary which tells how he hunted duck on the Chicago River during his lunch hour. Elijah's son, C.D. Peacock, incorporated the firm and gave it his name. It has occupied six locations since its founding, and survived the fire only because its vault was undamaged. The rest of the store was burned to the ground. The walls of the present store are of Verda antique marble, imported from Italy. C.D. Peacock III is the president, and C.D. Peacock IV works there, too. Altogether, there are three male Peacocks presently employed by the company.

"A magazine article carried a story about a house that was saved during the Chicago fire of 1871 because its owner, a policeman, soaked rugs and blankets in his well and carried them up to his roof. It told how he tore up the boardwalk in front of his house and got all the leaves out of the way. Supposedly, the man even used a keg of cider to help douse the fire around his house. I think the thing sounds too far-fetched and is only a joke. Please let me know."—E.Q.B., Oak Lawn

The house still stands at 2121 Hudson Avenue. Any map of the fire will show you that the entire surrounding area was burned to the ground. Versions of the story started with a newspaper account 2 or 3 days after the fire. The tale was included for years in grammar school textbooks and teachers took their children to look at the house. Historical research and testimony from the family verified the story, all except the detail about the cider — which some historians list as fact, but others question. There was a keg in the cellar, the policeman's widow maintained in later years, but the owner didn't have to use it because there was plenty of water available.

"You recently had an item about the Potter Palmers. Is it true that they had a mansion with doors that couldn't be opened from the outside?"
—Richard Lortig

You are right. No door to the office at 1350 N. Lake Shore Dr. had a key and no doorknob could be turned on the outside. Even the owners had to be admitted by a butler and a couple of liveried footmen. It was more than a mansion, however. It was a castle. The Palmers built it in 1882 on a 100,060 square-foot lot and adorned its walls with one of the greatest art collections anywhere. The couple entertained three presidents and countless princes and princesses there. The inside was even more garish than the outside, demonstrating all the ornate taste that was called Victorian. The average citizen of Chicago finally got a tour of the place at 50 cents a head when it was finally torn down so it could be replaced by a 22-story apartment building.

*"Could you give me
some additional
information on Potter
and Bertha Palmer? My
girl friend and I just saw
their monument in
Graceland Cemetery
and were very
impressed. We thought
we were at the tomb of
a king and queen.'
—Margie Hutton,
River Grove*

You were, in a way. Potter Palmer reigned supreme in Chicago first as a merchant, then real estate investor and finally as hotel owner. His wife, Bertha Honore Palmer, was undisputed queen of Chicago society from her marriage until her death almost 50 years later in 1918. Potter Palmer started a dry goods store on Lake Street in 1852 and originated the "Palmer system," later known as the "Chicago system" of giving customers their money back if not satisfied. He sold out to Marshall Field's firm and bought a mile of frontage on then-squalid State Street. He developed it and rented the stores to merchants. He built a grandiose hotel, only to see it destroyed by the Chicago Fire 13 days after completion. He then rebuilt State Street and his hotel, making the latter so fire-proof that he offered a reward to anyone who could burn it down. His wife, a writer once summarized, was never upstaged. She led society in matters of art, jewelry, houses and politics.

Gangsters, Crooks and Criminals

"When I was a boy almost 40 years ago, I remember riding the Englewood elevated with my father and having him point out what he called a 'murder castle' on the corner of 63rd and Wallace Streets. Was there really such a place?"
—George Mueller

The "murder castle" at 63rd and Wallace belonged to none other than Dr. H.H. Holmes, who killed an estimated 150 people — most of them women — before he was hanged in 1896. The "castle" was a very ordinary three-story building from the outside, with Holmes' drug store occupying the ground floor. Inside, it was a different story. After a fire in 1893, he balked at letting insurance investigators into the building. When they did get in, they discovered a maze of windowless, soundproof rooms, some with poison gas outlets and some with electrical apparatus. Secret passages and stairs led to other rooms containing a dissecting table, a huge furnace, hoists, an acid bath, and chutes leading to a quicklime pit. Though fragmentary human remains were found, the quicklime obliterated most of the evidence. Found guilty of the murder of an associate in Philadelphia, Holmes confessed to 26 other killings before he was executed. The "murder castle" was torn down in 1938 to make room for a post office.

"While riding on the Diversey bus I overheard one elderly man tell another that one of the most dreadful murders in the history of Chicago took place in a building near Diversey Parkway and Hermitage Avenue. What happened there?"
—Arthur Thompson

Your fellow rider was referring to the Luetgert murder case, a classic in the field of American criminology. In 1897, Adolph Luetgert, a prosperous sausage manufacturer, was accused of killing his wife. Only her gold wedding ring and a small fragment of bone were recovered from a vat of caustic in Luetgert's sausage factory. Nobody knows how she died. Her disappearance was explained by only a few wisps of evidence. When Luetgert heard his sentence — life imprisonment — he laughed at the jury and said, "She will come back. Then you will see what fools you were." He was convicted on the slimmest corpus delecti ever established in a Chicago court. And it's said that it took many Chicagoans months to work up courage to eat another sausage.

"The papers ran an article about Emil Roeski, and how he was freed from Menard Prison after serving 66 years. Is that a record? I recall another Illinois man about 5 years ago who was finally freed after a very long sentence."—J.N. Arthur

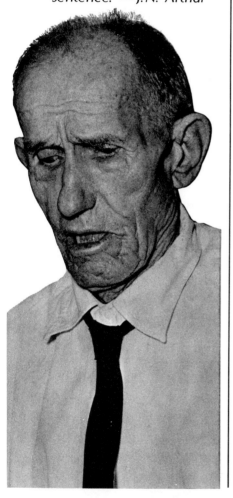

The man you recall is Richard Honeck. He served 64 years of a life sentence, also in Menard, and is the person listed in the Guinness Book of World Records under "longest sentences." The great tragedy of Emil Roeski is that he simply could not have been judged guilty in a modern court. He most probably committed no crime, and certainly was not sane. Roeski was associated with a vicious murdering gang known as the "car barn bandits," having been forced to join when he overheard their plans. Newspaper accounts described him as "half-witted," and "sleeping all the time." Jail officials described him as "too dull to have understood their plans." He was connected to only one of the murders. The other members despised Roeski; but even they denied his guilt, claiming they had set up Roeski to be killed in a tavern because of what he knew. The saloonkeeper, however, got in the way of the bullet meant for Roeski, and it was this shooting for which Roeski was convicted. An eloquent prosecutor and Roeski's close association with the hated car barn bandits helped convict him. Some doubt must have existed because Roeski alone was not hanged. Years later, he was finally judged insane and newspaper accounts as long ago as 1939 erroneously stated he had died in Menard.

"Can you tell me something about the 'Last Great Train Robbery' which occurred in the 1920s? I understand that it took place near a small town called Rondout which is near Libertyville, Ill."—Richard Deitos

Shortly before 10 p.m. on June 12, 1924, the Milwaukee Road's No. 57 was brought to a halt at Rondout by two gunmen — Brent Glasscock and Willie Newton. Waiting were four other gunslingers — Jesse, Willis and Joseph Newton, and Herbert Holliday, a former railroad man. They began shooting wildly and threw several tear gas bombs into the mail cars. In the melee, however, Glasscock mistakenly pumped five slugs into one of his comrades. The frightened and confused train crew was forced to carry 63 mail pouches, containing $2 million in loot, and the wounded man to the get-away cars. When Larry Benson, the railroad's police chief arrived on the scene in record time, he was met by another super-sleuth, postal inspector William Fahy. Fahy's evasive explanation got Benson thinking it might have been an inside job. His suspicions were vindicated when, thru a tip, the wounded gunman was found in a West Side hotel room. He confessed, naming Fahy and James E. Murray, a politician, as the masterminds.

"My grandfather, who I must confess has a rather over-active memory, has been telling me a lurid story of a love-triangle slaying which took place on the North Side when he was a boy. This case involved someone called 'The Ragged Stranger.' What's the real story?"—Ralph Small

"The Ragged Stranger" was a key figure in the bizarre double murder committed by ex-Army Lieutenant Carl Wanderer on June 1, 1920. Wanderer hired a skid row derelict to stage a fake holdup so the ex-soldier could impress his young wife. When the "ragged stranger" accosted the couple in the hallway of their home, Wanderer drew two pistols and shot his wife and the stranger. He then told police that his wife was killed by the robber, who was in turn slain by Wanderer. The "ragged stranger" was never identified. Later, Wanderer confessed the double slaying, saying he wanted to leave his pregnant wife for a 16-year-old typist. He was hanged on Sept. 30, 1921. As he stood on the gallows with the noose around his neck, he sang: "Old gal, old pal, you left me all alone . . ."

"I was told a weird tale about the Cook County Jail still having gallows waiting for a man who escaped years ago. Is this true?"—D.G.

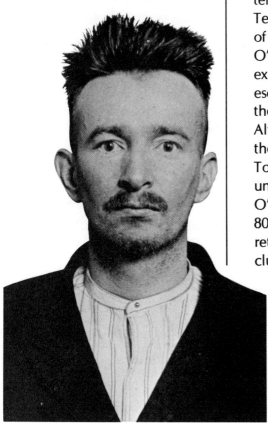

The gallows have been hanging around the County Jail for more than 50 years. Now they are in a storage room near the boiler in the Criminal Courts Building next to the jail. They were to be used for the execution of Tommy O'Connor, a Maxwell Street terrorist and killer, on Dec. 19, 1921. Terrible Tommy had been convicted of the murder of Detective Paddy O'Neil. Four days before the execution date, however, O'Connor escaped by slipping over the wall of the jail, then at 54 W. Hubbard St. Although he was never recaptured, the gallows were kept so Terrible Tommy could be "hanged by the neck until dead" if he ever turned up. O'Connor, who would be in his early 80s, probably would have his case retried if he ever did fall within the clutches of the law, we are told.

"Could you help me locate some addresses or places in Chicago that were made famous or notorious by gangsters? My boy friend is a nut about hoodlums in Chicago's past, especially Al Capone, and we would like to take a tour of such spots, even if they're only vacant lots now."
—Marilyn Sodoma

You have been made a tour guide. Start at:

• 2222 S. Wabash Ave., was once a saloon and brothel known as The Four Deuces. It was owned by Capone and was his first headquarters.

• 2126 S. Wabash Ave. was Colosimo's Restaurant. Capone's boss, Big Jim Colosimo, was murdered there on May 11, 1920.

• Heading north, you will cross the Illinois Central underpass at North Michigan Avenue and East Randolph Street, where on June 9, 1930, Jake Lingle was shot to death. He was a newspaper reporter in the employ of Capone.

• The 700 block on North State St. is a "must" for gangster historians. Dion O'Bannion, North side mobster boss, was gunned down in his flower shop at 738 N. State St., Nov. 19, 1924. His lieutenant, Little Hymie Weiss, was shot to death across the street, in front of Holy Name Cathedral, Oct. 11, 1926.

• The St. Valentine Day's massacre, a mass slaying of Bugs Moran's gang, took place Feb. 14, 1929, at 2122 N. Clark St. (continued)

- John Dillinger met his end in a fusillade in front of The Biograph Theater, which still stands at 2433 N. Lincoln Ave.
- The corner of North Cleveland Avenue and West Oak Street was the favorite location for gangland slayings — 15 of them occurred there.
- The Hawthorne Inn, in Cicero at 4823 W. 22nd St. (Cermak Rd.), became famous when Capone's rivals riddled it with machine gun bullets in an attempt to murder him, Jan. 12, 1925. Both he and his underlings escaped injury, however.
- Not so lucky was Johnny Torrio, Chicago's top gangster at the time, who was shot 12 days later in front of his home at 7011 S. Clyde Ave. He survived, but got the message and retired.
- Roger (The Terrible) Touhy ended his days in front of his sister's house at 125 N. Lotus Ave., Dec. 16, 1959, the victim of a shotgun blast.

"During the Roaring Twenties did gangsters really carry submachine guns around in violin cases, or was that just a myth Hollywood made up? It seems that it would be a pretty theatrical thing to do."—Steve G. Smith

Well, there were a lot of dance bands in those days before radio came along and maybe it was tough for the police to tell the difference between a gangster and a musician. The violin case was the most convenient thing for carrying the Thompson .45 caliber submachine gun with its bulky drum magazine. That was the way Machine Gun Jack McGurn, Al Capone's expert triggerman, did it. Vincent Gebardi — McGurn's real name — left boxing to take up killing on Feb. 15, 1927, when he bumped off one of the hoods who killed his father — a small-time alky cooker — the year before. His skill in eliminating the rest of the mob won him a chance to get into the big time, and he finally worked for Capone. It is believed that this maestro of the machine gun was the logistician of the St. Valentine day massacre. He was indicted for the crime, but the case never came to trial. A dapper dresser and a vicious killer, McGurn remained an underworld enforcer until Feb. 15, 1936, when he was murdered — gangland style — in a Milwaukee Avenue bowling alley. He was 38 and had been in the business as a killer for exactly 9 years.

"Could Action Line clear up once and for all whether those were bullet holes in the cornerstone of Holy Name Cathedral before the building was renovated in 1970? I've heard that a gangster was mowed down there with a machine gun, but I don't believe it."—R. Holbrook

On Oct. 11, 1926, "Little Hymie" Weiss was rubbed out almost on the doorstep of Holy Name Cathedral. He and four other mobsters had gotten out of their car to go to the flower shop across the street that served as the Weiss headquarters, when they were gunned down by a spray of machine gun bullets from a nearby rooming house. Little Hymie and his chauffeur were killed, the other three wounded. Altogether, 38 bullets were fired. Some of them tore away part of the cathedral's cornerstone, which was repaired. The two holes directly above the cornerstone for many years afterwards weren't made by flying lead—they were made by screws which held an old plaque announcing the time of masses.

"I just came to this country from Italy and I've been told that a local gangster, 'Diamond Joe' Esposito, might have been one of my relatives. Can you dig up some facts on him so that I might determine if there is any connection?"
—Mrs. R. P., Oak Park

Joseph Esposito, born in Accera, Italy, on April 28, 1872, arrived in New York in 1898 looking for the goldpaved streets. He found success after moving west to Chicago in 1905 by becoming political czar of Chicago's then infamous 19th Ward. Diamond Joe was assassinated on March 21, 1928, while walking between two of his bodyguards in the midst of one of our then turbulent elections. The politician was survived by his wife and three children. He was buried in opulence: a $3,200 bronze coffin and 57 cars rented at ($1,111) for the funeral, 26 of the cars to carry flowers. More than 8,000 people attended the rites. The lavishness didn't, however, match those of the people whom Esposito would eventually rest with: Dion O'Bannion, whose casket cost $10,000; Angeleno Genna, whose friends went the O'Bannion crowd "one grand better" for an $11,000 coffin and Michael Merlo, head of the Unione Sicilione, whose followers placed a $25,000 wax effigy of him in the cortege.

"Didn't Al Capone have his headquarters at some hotel just south of the Loop? If so, is it still standing?"—F.L., Oak Park

The hotel was and is the Metropole at 2300 Michigan Avenue. Fact and fiction intertwine in the stories about Capone's days in Chicago and his connection with the Metropole. Supposedly, Elliott Ness once drove a parade of confiscated beer trucks past Capone's window there. While it sounds like a publicity-seeking stunt that Ness would have pulled, our search failed to verify the story. Capone also had offices in a hotel connected by tunnel to the Metropole.

"Can you tell me what ever happened to the building where the St. Valentine's Day massacre occurred? I know a guy who has a brick from the wall where the gangsters stood when they were shot."—E.H.

The mass slaying occurred at 2122 N. Clark St., in the Werner Storage building. When the structure was razed in the 1960s, the bricks were sold to hundreds of collectors.

"I came to America from England in 1923. If I remember right, there were a number of dog tracks around the Chicago area, one of which was in the 31st Street and Cicero Ave. area. My friends will not believe me. Back up my memory."—Corby

Leave it up to a transplanted Englishman to give Chicago history lessons. One of the first dog tracks was started near Maywood in 1927 by gangster George (Bugs) Moran. Al Capone opened the Hawthorne Kennel Club the following year on the present site of Sportsman's Park. Half a dozen tracks, mostly run by hoodlums, sprouted up in the Chicago area, flourishing until 1931, when the Supreme Court outlawed the galloping Greyhounds in Illinois. Scarface Al's club was finally converted to horse racing as the National Jockey Club. It's president, Edward J. O'Hare, was later assassinated at Ogden Ave. and Rockwell St. on Nov. 8, 1939. His slaying was never solved.

"Could you find out for me where Al Capone lived in Chicago? A cousin of mine says it was in the 7200 block of South Prairie Ave. and that he remembers police cars being parked in front of it when he was a kid. I say it was the Metropole Hotel at 2300 S. Michigan Ave. Did he perhaps move and actually live in both places?"
—Sidney Delaney

Al Capone's Chicago residence was indeed 7244 S. Prairie Ave. His offices were in the Metropole Hotel. His first Chicago address — or at least the one he gave police when he was arrested in 1922, was at 2222 S. Wabash Ave., the Four Deuces brothel. One of the professions he claimed for himself was real estate salesman, so it is not surprising to find him investing in a summer home in Mercer, Wis., and a palatial estate in Miami Beach. His income in 1927 was estimated to be $105 million. In 1937, his wife was able to save his Miami home from being sold for taxes by coming up with the necessary $18,000. Capone was in prison and not selling much real estate at the time.

"Has anyone ever escaped from County Jail? I recently visited there and don't believe it's possible."—L.L., Elk Grove

Thousands have plotted it. Hundreds have tried and a few dozen have succeeded. No sooner was the place built in 1929 than six prisoners escaped by smashing an unbarred window after they had overpowered a guard. Easier escapes, however, have been made from the city jail (Bridewell), the state's attorney's headquarters in the jail, the courts themselves, the hospital (Cook County or the one in the jail) and in at least one case, the morgue. Most escapees from County Jail have been captured immediately. Others have been shot to death or broke arms, legs, ankles or in other ways injured themselves. Other attempts have been foiled before anyone got near the walls, as inspections uncovered hacksaw blades, weapons and holes cut into ventilation shafts. The No. 1 factor in successful escapes has been negligence — if not complicity — by guards. The percentage of failures would indicate it isn't worth it unless you're going to be in there forever, and, even then, it's questionable.

Politics and
Politicians

"Could you tell us how Bathhouse John, the famous 1st Ward alderman, got his name? Also, when did he die?"—Greg Horst, Lincolnwood

Ald. John J. Coughlin, known as "Bathhouse John" or simply "The Bath," earned his moniker by working in the old Palmer House turkish bath and later by owning two bathhouses before entering the city council in 1892. He and fellow 1st Ward alderman, Michael (Hinky Dink) Kenna, reportedly garnered millions from vice and gambling in their bailiwick. The figures came from no less a source than Minna Everleigh, madam of the city's most famous brothel. Whatever he made, however, Bathhouse John managed to squander on clothes, horses, and a good time. When he died in 1938, after 46 years in the city council, he was broke.

"Could you find out something for me about Chicago's late Ald. Michael (Hinky Dink) Kenna? I've often quoted his famous line about 'sticking to the small things when you're on the take.' The comment was made, I believe, when he and John (Bathhouse John) Coughlin stood up and voted against the city being sold down the river to Charles T. Yerkes, a traction magnate, who wanted to grab the Chicago streetcar franchise. I'd like to know if Hinky Dink's philosophy worked. How much was he worth when he died?"—R.H., Park Ridge

Actually, the advice was given to Kenna and Coughlin, and apparently taken. Kenna's estate totaled $1,023,22.67 after his death in 1946 at the age of 90. It may have profited him considerably during his life, but it didn't help much after his death. He left $33,000 for a mausoleum for his body and that of his wife. However, some of the heirs balked, and his grave finally got an $85 tombstone.

"While looking through some old books, I came across this card between the pages. I would like to know if it is worth any money and also who was William Lorimer and when was he in politics."—C.J. Picardi, Bellwood

Bill Lorimer was a legend in turn-of-the-century politics. Known as the "Blond Boss of Cook County," he rose from streetcar conductor to United States senator before his ultimate ruin. Lorimer was congressman from 1895 to 1901 and from 1903 to 1909. The electioneering card you found is probably from the first time he ran. Lorimer gained national repute in 1909 when he was suddenly elected United States senator by the state legislature (there was no direct election then) after four months of fruitless wrangling. Chicago newspapers howled in protest and began a relentless pursuit of Lorimer. Finally, in 1912, he was ousted from the Senate when it was proved that he was elected by corrupt means. He retired into private life and died in 1934. Your souvenir is not valuable, except as a keepsake.

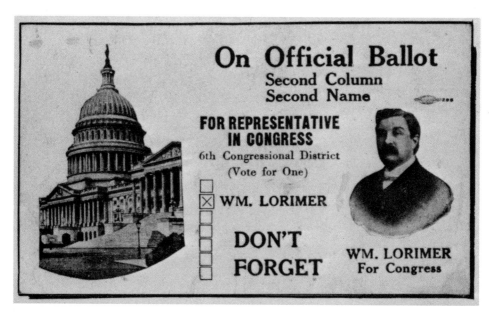

On Official Ballot
Second Column
Second Name

FOR REPRESENTATIVE IN CONGRESS
6th Congressional District
(Vote for One)

☒ WM. LORIMER

DON'T FORGET

WM. LORIMER
For Congress

"I've just heard an incredible story. It is that, during the 1920s, the mayor of Chicago went on an expedition to the south seas to look for a tree-climbing fish. If this is true, it is more preposterous than sending city commissioners and their wives to view Japanese garbage disposal. Can you confirm?"—
Dick Hildebrand

Only one person in Chicago's political history could pull such a stunt with complete aplomb, and that was William Hale Thompson, better known as "Big Bill." In 1924, he was out of office, and he and his cronies at the Fish Fan Club wracked their brains for a scheme to get him into the public eye. Thompson finally hit upon an astonishing idea. He would form an expedition to scour the south seas for a leggy fish which would get out of the water, jump 3 feet and climb cypress trees. Naturally, an obliging cypress wood industry built the ex-mayor a magnificent ketch and christened it the "Big Bill." His own face was carved into the oaken figurehead. The dauntless craft was launched that summer at Riverview amid impassioned oratory and cheering throngs. Shakedown cruises on the lake turned into beer parties for Bill's gang, and the trip almost never did get under way. True to form, most of the public figures involved (including Thompson) left the ship before it got to New Orleans. The captain of the staunch vessel, deprived of his passengers and his pay, settled in Panama and rented the boat out to fishermen to make ends meet. Big Bill never snared a tree-climbing fish, but he did get back into the limelight, and everyone had a wonderful time.

"We were having a discussion on mayoral elections. I said that Big Bill Thompson once rode a horse into the City Council chamber, and that it helped get him elected. The other people didn't believe me. Can you tell me what year it was and possibly turn up a picture?"—Hattie Malone

We don't believe your memory either, but then it's not 100 per cent wrong either. Mayor Thompson brought part of his campaign "circus" into the council chambers on Feb. 13, 1931, to enhance his cowboy image. He didn't ride the horse himself, however. He had dropped out of school and spent several years in the West, a fact that he milked for its political worth. He also once rented 50 jackasses as symbols of his Democratic opponents, but spared the council chambers the animals' presence. His antics went for nothing in 1931. He lost to Anton Cermak.

"All the fanfare a few years ago about Paul Powell and the money he made out of politics and left in shoeboxes led me into a discussion and argument with a Republican friend. Can you find out just how much Big Bill Thompson, the former Chicago mayor, was worth when he died?"—Ralph Conray

At his death, Big Bill's assets amounted to $2,103,024, of which $1,488,250 was in cash (gold certificates of $50, $100, $500 and $1,000 denominations). In the "cash laying around" department, Big Bill outdid Paul Powell, Illinois' former Secretary of State.

"Could you please find a picture of Mayor Daley when he was a young man? My aunt knew him then and kept an old photo, but she lost it. She was trying to describe him to us and went to get the picture, but it was gone. Please. We want to know what he looked like."— Kate and Janet

Would you believe the late movie actor, William Bendix? At least that's how his graduation picture turned out. Or would you rather a cherub? An altar boy photo does that for him. Most of the other pictures in our files show him with a smaller waist line, more hair, and less of a smile, but otherwise looking much the same as he does today.

"I have a bet with two friends that Mayor Daley at one time was a confirmed Republican. Nobody will believe me, but I know he was."—Lee Kampen, Hillside

On Nov. 3, 1936, Richard J. Daley ran as a write-in candidate for the Illinois General Assembly on the Republican ticket. The seat he won was left vacant by Republican David R. Shanahan, who had died just before the election. Another write-in candidate contested the election on the basis that Daley was not a Republican, but a member of the Cook County Democratic organization. The candidate also charged that the Democrats had conspired to keep his own name off the regular ballot, thus permitting the highly unusual maneuver. Daley, however, was seated in the House and permitted, on a motion from the then Democrat Ben S. Adamowski, to sit on the Democratic side of the aisle in Springfield. Adamowski later switched to the Republican party and ran against Daley for mayor.

Tragedies

"Two of my cousins brought up the topic of the Eastland disaster, in which so many people died when the ship capsized in the Chicago River. The pair have a bet on which way the boat flipped over — toward the river or toward the pier. Me? I sided with the cousin who said it tipped toward the pier because of the number of passengers boarding it. — Who is right?"—Diane C.

Looks like you cast your lot with a loser. On July 24, 1915, the passenger vessel, which was to carry 2,000 festive Western Electric employees on a picnic to Michigan City, Ind., toppled over on its port side — which was toward the river. The reason was partly that crowds had gone to that side to watch another boat and also to wave good-bye, but the principal cause was that the crew, in emptying the ballast tanks to get more passengers aboard, unbalanced the ship. The disaster, which took place at the foot of Clark Street, claimed the lives of 812.

"A recent mention of the Eastland tragedy jogged my memory about an equally calamitous shipwreck in Lake Michigan, I believe, in the 1800s off the Waukegan shore. Can you fill me in on it?"—D.W.

Prior to the Eastland, the wreck of the Lady Elgin held the ignominious record of being the worst disaster in the Great Lakes. The ship, an elegant sidewheel steamship, was carrying home a group of Milwaukee people from a Stephen A. Douglas political rally in Chicago on the night of Sept. 8, 1860. During a violent storm, the Lady Elgin was rammed by an unlit lumber schooner, the Augusta. Though the Augusta continued sailing for Chicago, the Lady Elgin began taking on water, snuffing out her boilers, and she was doomed. More than 300 passengers lost their lives trying to fight the lashing waves. Edward Spencer, a Northwestern University student, was immortalized by the school when he deliriously muttered, "Did I do my best?" after he had risked his life 17 times by swimming out to the ship to rescue as many people. Loose maritime laws later prompted an inquiry board to rule that nobody was at fault, but the Augusta's captain, D.M. Malott, and his crew paid. The Augusta's name was changed, but seamen refused to sign on. The ship finally was wrecked, and Malott and his men, aboard another craft, were all later lost in still another disaster.

"I've been trying to find out what play was on the bill when the Iroquois Theater burned down many years ago. Also, who was the star and why was the fire so bad?"—O. Zimmerman

Billed as "absolutely fireproof", the Iroquois Theater, located on the present site of the Oriental Theater, caught fire on Dec. 30, 1903, about 3:30 p.m. The musical "Mr. Blue Beard" was heralded as a "delight for children," and women and children comprised about 75 per cent of the over-capacity crowd. During the second act a drape, stirred by a breeze, caught fire when it touched an arc lamp. Flames filled the stage. Eddie Foy, the star, ordered the so-called asbestos curtain dropped, but it caught halfway and remained there. It burned. A strong draft then flowed beneath the partly lowered curtain from a stage door opened by fleeing actors, carrying a great ball of flame into the audience. Many died in their seats, others were trampled. Bodies were found piled high in front of the exit doors that were locked despite city ordinances. The 603 victims included 212 children. Five city and theater officials were indicted for sins of commission and omission, but there was no legal punishment. The tragedy did, however, produce a number of our current fire regulations.

Fire Marshal James Horan had little to do but flood the back lots of Chicago for skating rinks in the days before Dec. 22, 1910, when he leaped out of bed at 4:09 a.m. to answer the alarm. He and 23 other men - most of them fire fighters - were crushed under a falling wall at the blaze in Morris & Co.'s meat storage house. The chief and his men were clearing a loading platform, trying to get at the fire in a basement, when the wall fell. Rescuers, guided by Horan's white helmet, found the chief's body the next day in a sitting position, arms folded across his face and nary a bruise on it. Horan's skull was fractured, however. It was, by far, the largest loss of life the Chicago Fire Department ever suffered. The cause of the fire was unknown and the property damage was estimated at $750,000.

"There's an old-timer who hangs around the corner tavern and wins drinks with his fantastic memory. His latest is that about 50 years ago, a blimp fell through the roof of a downtown bank. Everyone else laughed and gave the old man terrific odds, but I thought I would get a little inside dope from you."—Terry O'Malley

Hold on to your money. On July 21, 1919, the blimp Wingfoot Express caught fire above the Loop and plunged through the skylight of the Illinois Trust and Savings Bank, now the Continental Illinois National Bank and Trust Company, killing 13. The 158-foot craft took off earlier from White City Amusement Park on the South Side and was about 1,500 feet over the financial district when the fire broke out. Of two passengers and three crewmen, only the pilot and a mechanic parachuted safely. Out of control, its 90,000 cubic feet of hydrogen burning fiercely, the airship tore through the bank roof. Flaming gasoline sprayed down on the bank's 100 employees, killing 10 and injuring 28.

"As every Lithuanian in Chicago knows, there is a monument at the corner of California Avenue and Marquette Road dedicated to two men killed in a trans-Atlantic flight back in 1933. My father maintains that the men were actually shot down by the Nazis, a fact that came to light after the war. No one else among our friends or relatives could confirm this or remembers anything about it. Could you help?"—S.M.

There is some support for the theory that Stephen Darius and Stanley Girenas were shot down. Both fliers were Chicagoans of Lithuanian birth. Their goal was to fly from New York City to establish a flight record. It was also to be a good will gesture between Lithuanians in this country and their homeland. The flight ended over a forest in Germany, alledgedly because the plane ran out of fuel. The Nazis, however, had been alarmed earlier when the plane flashed a searchlight over a "labor camp" attempting to find a landing place. A Lithuanian doctor told an interviewer in 1946 that he had prepared the bodies for burial and both bore bullet holes. His statements have never been confirmed, however.

"The father of a buddy of mine used to be a deputy sheriff in Lake County. His favorite subject is student demonstrations and he says they all ought to be handled the same way the sheriff ended the Fansteel sit-down strike back in 1937. He claims they used a clever tower on the back of a truck to drive the workers out of the plant. Please give me details because I don't think it was as glorious as he claims."
—Richard Manners, Evanston

If he thinks that tear gas and nauseating gas are somehow glorious, we doubt you're going to change his mind. You might remind him that an earlier tear gas attack by "his side" failed to dislodge the strikers. The sit-in was the result of the firm refusing to recognize a CIO union. The sit-down strike was a desperate, and sometimes effective, weapon by workers in a time when even a short strike could mean actual hunger within a few days. The tower was mounted on the back of a truck and the gas was shot out of slots in it. It sickened the men and broke the back of the strike.

"While I was overseas in World War II a story was circulating about a crucifixion in Chicago It supposedly made all the headlines in 1945 or 1946, but I haven't been able to track down the tale. Can you supply me with a lead?"—James Cacini

Frederick Walcher's moans and sobs led police to a grisly scene beneath the elevated tracks at 1637 Clybourn Ave. on the morning of March 9, 1945. Walcher, then 48, was found nailed to a crude wooden cross. Three-inch spikes were driven through his hands, while his body was affixed with a rope so that his weight wouldn't tear the flesh. On his head was a rosette of twigs resembling the crown of thorns. The Austrian-born janitor, a Bund sympathizer, admitted he had arranged the stunt with a group of accomplices to focus attention on his plan for a Fascistlike "American Industrial Democracy," a mixture of totalitarian politics and economics. Doctors were amazed, noting that the spikes were driven through Walcher's palm by someone with knowledge of anatomy, since they avoided any vital blood vessels. Walcher got his "million dollars worth of publicity" and all it cost him, besides the pain, was a $100 fine plus costs for disorderly conduct.

"If I recall right, back in the late '40s or early '50s, there was a Green Hornet streetcar and a gasoline truck involved in an accident in which there were quite a few deaths. I think this took place in the vicinity of the Loop. No one I talk to seems to recall it. Could you get us the date and other pertinent information?"—Richard Wysocket, Stickney

You were off merely on the location. The accident occurred at 63rd and State Streets. It happened May 25, 1950, and took the lives of 34 people, injuring another 50. The streetcar, supposed to turn around because an underpass was flooded, apparently had been going too fast, and crashed into the gasoline truck. The driver of the streetcar and 33 passengers were burned to death, many of them because the back door of the Green Hornet jammed shut and the passengers panicked trying to open it. Some did escape through a small window. The driver had been involved in 10 accidents in the preceding year. The holocaust was described at the time as the nation's worst disaster involving a motor vehicle.

"I'd like some information about Our Lady of the Angels School fire which took so many lives. When did it occur and what caused it?"—Marion Giemsoe

The Dec. 1, 1958 holocaust was the worst school fire in Chicago's history. The cause has never been definitely established. A 13-year old boy had confessed to starting the tragic fire, but in March, 1962, a judge found him not guilty on the grounds that evidence to substantiate his confession was lacking. Supposedly kindled in a pile of rubbish in the basement, the blaze roared through the building like a volcano eruption while afternoon classes were in session. In some classrooms, children died seated at their desks, overcome by smoke, while many leaped from second-floor windows. The fire claimed the lives of 92 pupils and three nuns. The archdiocese eventually paid $3.2 million in damages, whether or not parents had filed lawsuits. While the retelling of the story over the years has reopened wounds for those involved, it also has resulted in greater safety precautions and measures in the schools and helped to ward off similar tragedies.

Streetcars, Buses, and the Elevated

"When were horse-drawn streetcars discontinued in Chicago? A friend of mine has a street car watch and this is the only way he can ascertain the timepiece's approximate age."—Sue Grider

Horses received their pink slips July 1, 1906, after trolley wires were finally installed in the Loop. A unique situation had prevailed up to then. By 1900, all the West Side horse car lines had been converted to either cable or electric power. The Harrison Street car ran on electricity from Western Avenue, went up to Clinton Street, then to Adams and over to State Street. A city ordinance, however, restricted trolley wires in the Downtown area, and a team of horses had to be hitched to the car at Wells Street (then 5th Avenue) for the rest of the trip. Otherwise, horses were doing most of the pulling in the early morning hours, when the 94 miles of cable had to be drawn into various power houses for daily inspection.

"How long have the 'L' tracks been up in Chicago?"— R. Longden, Westmont

More than 80 years. The oldest is the stretch between the Loop and 39th Street on the north-south "L". It was originally built in 1892. Cars were pulled by a 26-foot, coal-burning locomotive. The structure was continued to Jackson Park in 1893 for the World Columbian Exposition. The Lake Street and Logan Square "L" structures were also built during the 1890s, while the Evanston and Ravenswood tracks were completed a decade later.

"I recently saw a booklet put out by the CTA showing the old buses and streetcars used in Chicago. The one that fascinated me the most was a funeral streetcar that apparently was used here between 1910 and 1919. Could you find out more about it?"—Richard T. Tibbs

The car you saw is one of two used during that period. There was also an elevated funeral car that served the city between 1905 and 1932. Cemeteries at that time were quite a ways by horse or early model automobile. The elevated lines had elevators at the Hoyne and Laflin stops on the Douglas Park line to lift the casket up to the platform. Elsewhere, it was up to the pallbearers to do the work. Track connections could be made with the Aurora and Elgin line and there was a spur going into the Mount Carmel and Oak Ridge cemeteries. Others served directly by the western line were Waldheim and Concordia cemeteries. Mourners rode in the same car with the casket, with regular streetcars or extra elevated cars being attached for large funerals.

"Can you tell me when the open-air double decker bus was introduced here? I remember when they were retired during the 1930s, but I'm not quite old enough to recall when they were first used. If you could, please print a picture to show the kids of today what they missed."—
Mrs. Sam Gavrilis

If you had 10 cents and a hearty constitution back in 1917, you could climb to the upper deck of Chicago's first "fresh air taxi." In spite of their ability to make a Spartan sob in the wintertime, the open top double-deckers ran for 20 years and were retired (appropriately enough) on a chilly Dec. 27, 1937. The closed-top models carried on gamely enough until 1950, when they too bit the dust.

"Could you help some guys down in the composing room out with some information? We've had a big argument going. When did they start building the State Street subway and when did they dedicate it?"—Composers

Chicago planners dreamed of a subway for decades, finally began to build it Dec. 17, 1938. It was finished five years later, Oct. 17, 1943. The Dearborn Street subway, which had been started in early 1939, was not completed until 1951 because of material shortages in World War II. In the interim, Chicagoans were able to take guided tours of the subway work and hear the tunnels compared to the wondrous caverns that are tourist attractions elsewhere. Any comparison between stalactites and stalagmites and the oozing mud beneath Chicago, however, was built on an over worked imagination.

P.C.C. cars (Blue Gooses prior to 1946) had a top cruising speed of about 47 m.p.h., according to the CTA, with possibilities of slightly over 50 m.p.h. under favorable conditions. The Lake Street "L" chap, however, was probably right, as he, prior to 1949, would have made 16 stops in that stretch with a car capable of 35 m.p.h. San Francisco's P.C.C. cars, we're told, have the same electrical equipment as Chicago's.

Weird and Eerie Tales of Chicago

"I've heard a spooky story about a fireman's handprint that is still on a firehouse window to this very day. Nobody could erase it after the man died in a fire. Is this true or simply another legend?"—G.G.

True is the story. Fireman Francis X. Leavy was washing windows of the Engine Co. 107 Firehouse at 2258 W. 13th St. on Good Friday, April 18, 1924, when an alarm interrupted him. Curran's Hall was ablaze on 14th Street and Blue Island Avenue, and Leavy told his captain that he would finish the pane when he returned. Leavy and his comrades, however, never returned. With the fight won, the men trudged wearily down a fire escape. Then a section of wall and roof caved in. The next morning another fireman resumed the dead man's domestic chores and found Leavy's hand print etched on the unfinished window. Firemen thereafter claimed that even water, soap and ammonia couldn't obliterate the ghostly reminder. The evidence didn't last: The window was broken in 1946 by a newsboy who chucked a paper through it.

"Can you solve the mystery of Peabody's tomb for all of us here at work? Mr. Peabody supposedly is encased in a glass coffin located in a cemetery maintained by monks near Oak Brook, Ill. In the discussion, it was mentioned that the monks guard the grounds at night with dogs, and if someone is caught, the person is detained in the chapel and forced to pray the entire night. These stories seem popular with people of high school and college age, so please come up with the facts."
—Edward Pieszchola

The source of these wild tales that are indeed rampant in the Western suburbs is the little Portiuncula chapel and mausoleum on the grounds of St. Joseph Franciscan Seminary in Oak Brook. The small church, a replica of the chapel which St. Francis of Assisi rebuilt and in which he eventually died, was constructed by Francis Peabody's widow on the spot where her husband, the coal magnate, died of a heart attack in 1922. His and his son's bodies are interred there. There is no glass coffin and the bodies are not, as one version has it, "floating in oil." Vandals—of the high school and college variety—have done an estimated $10,000 damage to the little church, and the Franciscan Friars turn trespassers over to police.

"Ever since I read a biography of Harry Houdini, I've been intrigued by the idea that one of his greatest exploits took place here in Chicago after he had begun debunking fake spirit mediums. He and a photographer from the old Evening American took a picture during a seance that was so sensational that it was reproduced four columns wide in the paper sometime during 1926. Is that picture still in the files? I'd like to see it."—
G. Van Vuren

We did you one better. We located a person who attended that seance in 1927. We were having trouble finding the picture in our files, so we asked Tony Berardi Sr., former CHICAGO TODAY chief photographer, if he happened to remember it. His face lit up like a cherry blossom. He recalled every detail and helped us find the paper in which the photo appeared. Houdini had arranged the debunking. The photographer, Al Struck, sneaked a camera into the seance in a physician's bag. Berardi's job was to loosen a nail holding a window shut so his compatriot and camera could flee as soon as the picture was taken. The medium, Mrs. Minnie Reichert, 6747 S. Emerald Ave., had earlier conjured up the photographer's sister, and the long dead Indian Chief Black Hawk supposedly was talking at the time of the photo. She had assured everyone, before the lights were extinguished, that she did not touch or use the voice-projecting trumpet during the seance. Fortunately, Berardi also was a boxer and was able to convince the woman and her three-inch fingernails to stay her distance afterwards.

"My grandfather likes to tell tales from the 'good old days,' but his last one left me hanging for more. He told me of a miracle that occurred here in Chicago in the early 1930s. Seems there was a mysterious religious image on a building that attracted many, many people. He could not recall all the details and even grandmother thought it happened years later. What can you tell me?"—S.M.

Your grandfather's right. In early July, 1931, the 6-day wonder of the West Side — a figure of a mother and child — appeared nightly on the wall of an apartment building at 1107 S. Ashland Ave. A pragmatic police lieutenant, weary of directing a 50-man force to control the crowd of 20,000 who went to kneel and pray, ended the miracle on July 16. In a touch of irony, his search led to the apartment of Peter Genna, the infamous leader of the Genna liquor gang. What the policeman found was an arc lamp throwing beams upon a bay window in the Genna home. The window pane, in turn, with the help of curtain fringe, cast an image that could be construed as the Virgin Mary and Child. When the officer pulled the shade down, the silhouette disappeared, and so did the disappointed crowd, complete with peanut and hot dog vendors who cashed in on the "miracle".

Buildings and Architecture

"When I was knee-high to a grasshopper, I was told that the present Coliseum was actually Libby Prison of the Civil War days. It was supposedly brought here from the South and rebuilt as a convention hall for the Columbian Exposition in 1893. If all this is true, then the Coliseum is a much more interesting building than I thought."—H.M. Schooley, Burlington

The Coliseum, one of Chicago's most famous buildings, is not itself the Confederacy's Libby Prison, which held 45,000 Union soldiers during the Civil War. The castle-like wall on Wabash Avenue, however, is part of the original enclosure for the prison. Libby Prison came to Chicago in 1888, when a group of Chicago business men hit upon the plan of using it to house a Civil War museum. Transported here at a cost of $200,000, the prison's 600,000 numbered stones were reassembled at the site between 14th and 16th Streets on Wabash Avenue. By 1897, the museum wasn't making enough money to make ends meet, so Libby Prison was razed and the Coliseum built in 1899.

"I would like to find a picture of the old federal building and post office on South Dearborn Street. I thought you might have one in your files."—Anton Soucek

We got the picture out to send you and spent so much time reminiscing about that building that we thought we'd print a copy so others could do the same. It was once perhaps Chicago's most dramatic, authoritative and yet, awkward structure. It is no more.

"I happen to like to look at old mansions. I've heard that there are supposed to be some still standing around Prairie Avenue on the South Side. I would like to know where they are because the information I have is very vague."—Mrs. Susan Hester

The John J. Glessner Mansion at 1800 S. Prairie Ave. is open to the public. It is the best-known of the old houses that once lined Prairie Avenue, the most fashionable street in Chicago in the late 1800s. The 35-room mansion was designed by Henry Hobbs Richardson in 1886 and is believed to have had a strong influence on architect Louis Sullivan and his famous pupil, Frank Lloyd Wright. The owner, John Jacob Glessner, was a director of International Harvester and lived in the house until 1936, long after most of Chicago's affluent had moved to the North Side. The mansion now belongs to the Chicago School of Architecture Foundation and is open to the public during the day except on Mondays and Wednesdays.

"Grandfather thinks he knows everything, but I believe that I've got him dead to rights this time. He says that Chicago is the site of the world's first skyscraper. I am sure that the first one must have been built in New York."—Mrs. S.W.

Sorry, but Gramps is right again. The world's first skyscraper was the 12-story Home Insurance Building, designed by William Le Barron Jenney and constructed at the corner of La Salle and Adams Streets in 1885. The term "skyscraper" does not only mean that a building has to be of a considerable height. It denotes a tall building constructed on a metal skeleton, with the steel framework supporting walls, floors, and ceilings. For years, there was some dispute whether the Home Insurance Building was a true skyscraper, in that the beams used for the construction were iron and some architects doubted the skeleton actually supported the building. They felt the walls, as in past structures, did the job. The question was settled in 1931, when the Home Insurance Building was razed to make way for the Field Building. A special architectural committee examined every step of the demolition and concluded that the Home Insurance Building was "the father of the modern skyscraper."

"Could you give me the name of the architect who designed the Carson Pirie Scott & Co. building in the loop? I need information on his background and other works for an art paper."—Laura Johnson

The name of Louis Sullivan is one which you'll run across very often in any book on architecture in Chicago. The Carson Pirie Scott & Co. Building is considered Sullivan's masterpiece and the "ultimate achievement of the First Chicago School." Fortunately, the architects who enlarged the structure in 1904 and again in 1960 respected Sullivan's original design and followed his patterns closely in their additions. The building today is therefore the result of several stages of construction, so the total building is less unified than it otherwise would have been. It was originally constructed in 1899 for the Schlesinger and Mayer Co., and purchased by Carsons in 1904. Sullivan came to Chicago in 1873 and was very influential in our building boom which followed the great fire.

"I have a dining room table which was designed (I was told when I bought it) by Frank Lloyd Wright, the famous architect. Could you find out if Mr. Wright did indeed design any furniture?"—Kathlyn D. Scott, Lake Villa

He most certainly did, and you can probably verify your table through the Chicago School of Architecture Foundation at 1800 S. Prairie Ave. Wright designed furniture because he believed in "organic architecture" and that furnishings should be one with the building. His furniture stressed the simple, building on straight lines and rectilinear forms. The foundation has a booklet on Wright's furniture, available for $2 a copy.

"You probably don't remember the Midway Gardens out at 60th Street and Cottage Grove Avenue. It was a pleasure dome designed by Frank Lloyd Wright and was torn down just before the Depression. Anyway, it was filled with beautiful sculpture, all designed by Wright himself. I wonder if you could find out if any of that sculpture was saved and can be seen today?"
—John Miller, Hillside

Midway Gardens, the fairyland of light and space which Wright designed in 1913, was a victim of cruel fate. Ahead of its time as a cultural and recreational center for the South Side, the gardens had become a dance hall and beer garden by the time the 1920s ushered in prohibition. From then on, it was all downhill for the block-long structure, and Wright was prompted to say, "Will some one in mercy not give them the final blow and tear them down?" His wish came true in October, 1929, - the month of the stock market crash. The statues of the sprites and other concrete sculpture which lined the gardens disappeared into private collections or were crushed beneath the wrecker's ball. None are available for public viewing today. However, those who wish to recapture Midway Gardens in its heyday can check the fine series of photographs which can be seen at the Chicago Architectural Photo Company, 75 E. Wacker Drive.

"It seems that every building they put up in Chicago is taller than the last. However, I remember when I was in high school, the late Frank Lloyd Wright proposed the ultimate in tall buildings. It was supposed to be a mile high. Could you tell me what happened to the idea?"
—Rita Jacowski

Wright's 5,280-foot building is as much of a dream today as when he proposed it in 1956. However, he never expected the "Illinois" to be built in his lifetime, or even shortly afterward. "But, if we're going to have centralization, why not quit fooling around and have it?" the venerable architect asked. The building, which was to get its stability from a "tap-root foundation" sunk deep in the earth, was expected to house 130,000 workers. Before beginning construction on a site near the Adler Planetarium and Astronomical Museum, Wright said he needed only a sponsor with 100 million dollars. No one came forward.

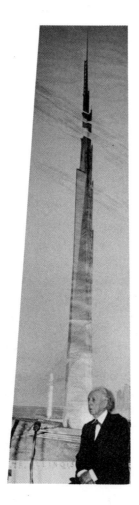

"Could you please find out what the apparatus is on top of the building at 737 N. Michigan Ave.? I'll bet millions of people have seen that thing and do not know what it is or who built it."
—O. G. Cummings

We talked to present and past tenants and owners, and finally confirmed that the Charles A. Chaplin family had it built in 1929 and lived for a very short time in the penthouse. The domed observatory was constructed for a member of the family who was an amateur astronomer. They lost it shortly afterward however, on a foreclosure. The telescope is gone and the stairway leading to it has been removed. The penthouse serves as offices for seven orthopedic surgeons and the dome houses the air conditioning equipment for the doctors' offices.

"Please help me answer my nephew's question. He was visiting Chicago and asked me what that 'funny looking dome' is on top the building next to Chicago Today newspaper. He spotted it from a downtown observation tower and made me promise to find out why it's there and what it's used for."
—Charles Tippin

The pear-shaped dome atop the Sheraton-Chicago Hotel is a relic of the building's origin in 1929 as the Medinah Athletic Club. It then had 400 rooms, a miniature golf course, two swimming pools, handball courts and a rifle range. After a mortgage foreclosure in the early 1930s it became a hotel. Sheraton bought it in 1948 and took down the 50-foot Medinah emblem adjoining the pear-shaped dome, which is not open to the public.

Nationalities

"Can you settle a verbal fracas? We've been arguing about the boundaries of a section of Chicago called 'Bucktown'. My friends claim it was the Division Street-Ashland Avenue area, while I believe it started farther north, like around Cortland Street. A dinner rides on your answer."
—Just Irene

"Bucktown" is the nickname for the area surrounded by Fullerton, Armitage, Western and Damen Avenues. According to old newspaper accounts, it was a tough Polish neighborhood back in the 1920s, when police would "tiptoe in bunches through the streets for mutual protection." Local residents, however, claim the area's wild reputation is undeserved and the neighborhood was not that rugged. The location was so named because many of the people living there owned bucks (he-goats).

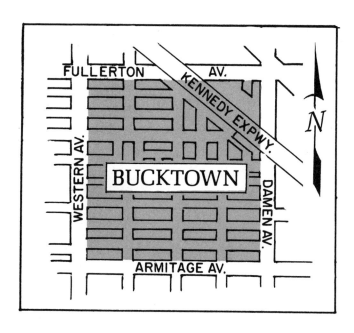

The Polish constitution of 1791 remained in effect for only one year, but a lot of freedom-seeking Poles fought and died for it. It was adopted during a quick Easter recess after three years of haggling by the national Sejm (assembly of nobles). The document recognized a hereditary monarchy, but more importantly it gave peasants protection under the law and opened land ownership and offices in the church and state to townspeople. Absolute religious toleration was established and further provision for reform was established by subsequent parliaments. Russia, Prussia, and Austria used the new constitution as an excuse to invade and partition the country. A ragamuffin army led by Thaddeus Kosciuszko and the king's nephew fought off the invaders successfully in battle after battle using pitchforks and scythes, but finally it was forced to surrender. The three larger nations each took a part of Poland, which was not reunited until 1918.

"We've heard of a Scandinavian community somewhere in the Chicago area called 'Andersonville.' Could you please tell us where this neighborhood is and how we would get there?"
—Mrs. La Verne Helgesen Evansville, Wis.

Andersonville, in the Foster Avenue-Clark Street section of Uptown Chicago, is renowned for its cleanliness and friendliness. It is also the place to go to sample Nordic food, candy, gifts, liquor, clothes, furniture, magazines and newspapers. Every morning at 10 a. m., a bell rings to remind merchants to sweep the sidewalks in front of their stores. On the first Saturday in October, Andersonville has its annual parade, with bands, floats, clowns, pretty girls, and Vikings. To get there, just take Interstate Route 90 to Foster Avenue and head east.

"Every Christmas in the Old Town area, people stage an outside procession with individuals dressed as Joseph and Mary (riding a burro); shepherds and the three wise men. What's the idea behind all this?"
—The Durbins

The event of which you speak is a Posada, Spanish for "inn." The pageant originated in Mexico when missionaries sought a way to tell the Christmas tale to people who couldn't read or write. Groups usually assemble at two fine Mexican restaurants—La Hacienda del Sol, 1945 N. Sedgwick St. and the Azteca Restaurant, 215 W. North Ave. The first group tours the neighborhood, ending at St. Michael's Church, 1633 N. Cleveland Ave., while the Azteca contingent visits a number of homes in the area and returns to the restaurant for carol singing and free hot tamales. If you'd like to join either group, check with one of the three places mentioned about two weeks before Christmas.

The River and the Lake

"How did Goose Island ever get its name? There's nothing but factories there now."
—Arthur Ludka

Goose Island was created in 1850, when the Chicago Land Company, while digging for clay, cut the channel which forms the eastern edge of the island in the north branch of the Chicago River. The place was originally called Ogden Island, after Mayor William B. Ogden, who owned part of the land company. Later, the island was settled by Irish-Americans, who immediately planted cabbage patches and brought in their geese. The Irish prevailed, and the name Goose Island stuck. As the city grew, and people moved out from its center, the area became the industrial site it is today. Sadly enough, there is probably not one goose left on the island.

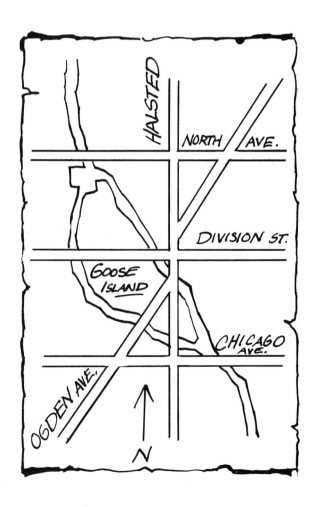

"When the flow of the Chicago River was reversed on Jan. 17, 1900, I'm told it involved 'a great race' against time and a kidnaping. What exactly happened?"
—W. Andrews

In 1885, raw sewage was being dumped either directly into Lake Michigan or into the Chicago River, which flowed into the lake. Drinking water intake pipes were extended farther into the lake. Undercurrents and wind shifts, however, made it a losing battle and Chicagoans were gagging on their own waste, which also was infecting them with typhoid fever. The state legislature then created the Metropolitan Sanitary District, giving engineers the task of reversing the flow of the river to carry the sewage downstream. On Jan. 2, 1900, the project was completed. St. Louis, however, objected to the fouling of its water and prepared to seek a federal court injunction to prevent the opening of the Bear Trap flood gates in Lockport. An independent commission of engineers had to approve the project and reported to the governor, who could then authorize the opening of the locks. Sanitary district officials sped to Springfield and to Joliet to collect the three commissioners, who were sleeping. Agreeing that the situation was desperate, the trio ordered the locks opened 16 minutes before St. Louis filed its suit.

> *"I've heard there's a sign on the locks between the Chicago River and Lake Michigan saying that the changing of the flow of the river is one of seven wonders of the modern world. I would like to find out what the other six are."*
> —Jeff McNulty

There are more than six. The honor, bestowed by the American Society of Civil Engineers, belongs to the sewage disposal system of Chicago, the key to which has been the reversal of the river. It is not considered a wonder of the world, but rather one of "the seven modern civil engineering wonders" in the United States. Our sewage system, however, is in prominent company because the other six chosen in 1954 were the Colorado River Aqueduct, Empire State Building, Grand Coulee Dam, Hoover Dam, Panama Canal and San Francisco Bay Bridge. Each year since then another has been added, including Gateway Arch in St. Louis, NASA Complex and J. F. K. International Airport in New York.

"Just when is the park district going to allow houseboats to be moored in their harbors? We can't seem to get a definite answer from them."
—R. W.

Houseboaters, a strange and romantic breed, usually get short shrift from the society they live in, probably because they don't pay taxes. Park District officials say they never want any part of them in the harbors and cite Rule 20 which says, "No houseboat shall be permitted in a harbor except in inclement weather, as a matter of refuge." During the Depression there were houseboat colonies in the north branch of the Chicago River at Irving Park Road and in Lake Calumet. The North Side colony was the Montmartre of Chicago, with students, artists, and writers dwelling in some of the 58 craft moored there. The rest of the population were simple folk who caused no trouble and wanted most of all to be left alone. The city, however, considered their floating homes hazards to navigation and polluters of our sparkling river. In the end, legal pressure and prosperity combined to finish off Boatville.

"My friend and I disagree on the history of Bubbly Creek. He was born west of Ashland Avenue and I was raised east of it. My friend claims Bubbly Creek never ran east of 39th Street and Racine Avenue. I maintain it ran east of Morgan back in the 1920s on what is now Pershing Road."
—Walt Monty

Phew! Do you bring up an odoriferous part of Chicago's history. Parts of Bubbly Creek have been filled in three times in response to the city's inability to hold its nose any longer. A branch of the Chicago River, the creek was used by the stockyards as a sewer outlet, getting its name from the gases which bubbled to the surface. In 1915, an intrepid reporter tried to row across it, but had to turn back when his boat was enveloped in a six-foot wide bubble that didn't smell like roses. In 1920, part of it was filled in, and the worst of the pollution eliminated. The branch you refer to (east to Halsted Street) was eliminated in 1937 and the southwestern branch was done away with as a result of an Act of Congress passed in 1959.

"After walking across the Michigan Avenue bridge on my way to work every day, I got to wondering if there is any kind of schedule for opening and closing them."
—R.T., Lisle

You might say the bridge schedule works in reverse. There is no specified time when they open and close, but there are hours when they do not open. Because a traffic tieup would occur during the rush hours if they were open, they may not be raised along the main river, the south branch to Roosevelt Road and the north branch to Ohio Street daily from 7:30 a.m. to 10 a.m. and from 4 p.m. to 6:30 p.m. and on Saturdays from 7:30 a.m. to 10 a.m., 12:30 p.m. to 2 p.m. and 5 p.m. to 6 p.m. Otherwise the bridges go up and down as river traffic demands. Twenty years ago, it cost roughly $20 to raise and lower a bridge, depending on size, and Port Authority officials guessed that it probably costs more than twice as much today.

"Do you know about the tunnel they're always talking about building between England and France? Well, my grandpa says an engineer once had a plan to bridge Lake Michigan. It doesn't seem like a bad idea. I wonder if you could tell me exactly where it was supposed to be - grandpa couldn't remember."
—*John Byrne*

The Lake Michigan bridge looks suspiciously like one of those plans thought up when they didn't have anything else to do during the Depression. This one was the brainchild of Leroy L. Hunter, and extended from 73rd Street in Chicago to Michigan City, Ind., 37 miles away. Landfill projects at either end would have been divided into lots and sold to finance construction. The new body of water formed by the concrete barrier was to be called "Lake Indiana." Amusingly enough, the project, plus rerouting the Chicago River and electrifying and rerouting all Chicago railroads would have cost a mere 200 million dollars, according to Hunter.

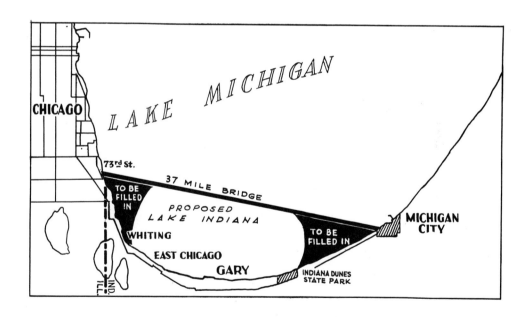

Actually, nothing. But the City Council had big plans for the man-made island prior to the 1933 World's Fair. City officials in 1919 passed an ordinance to build five islands along the lakefront, from Roosevelt Road to 56th Street, but the vision never materialized. The islands were to be several hundred feet off shore and connected with bridges to form a lakefront park. Northerly Island was the only one ever completed, unfortunately. The project was scrapped in 1937 for lack of funds. The island was expanded for the 1933 World's Fair and connected with the mainland afterward.

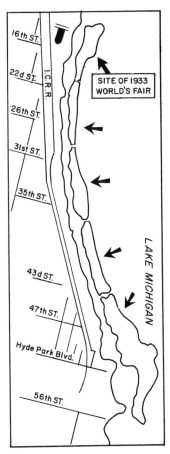

"We students at Harrington Institute at 410 S. Michigan Ave. have been wondering about the lighthouse on the south side of Navy Pier in the harbor. Who owns it, is it for sale, how could we get to see it?"
—Muffie Schumacher

For a lighthouse that has been at Chicago's front door since 1893, there is surprisingly little information about the Chicago Harbor Lighthouse (its official name). It is 82-feet high and the 81,312 candle power light can be seen for 24 miles. When the lighthouse was rebuilt in 1919, a prism lens from San Francisco was installed, which still is in use. The lighthouse is staffed by the Coast Guard, which reports it cannot conduct tours there because of the difficulty of getting on and off. Four men operate the light, working two weeks on, one week off. The Coast Guard, however, does have tours of its rescue stations at Calumet Harbor and Wilmette Harbor. Groups of up to 50 can make arrangements for tours at the Coast Guard office at 610 S. Canal St.

> *"Lake Michigan has seen many types of warships - from cruisers to submarines, but I wonder if anything like an aircraft carrier has ever sailed here? I heard that one did, and that it was the largest ship on the lakes, but it seems impossible."*
> —George Jackin, Westmont

Our lake has seen some of the most unlikely ships in the world, including its own two (yes, two) aircraft carriers. The Wolverine and the Sable were probably the only coal-burning, side-wheel ships ever to join the navy as flat-tops. Both originally were lake cruise ships - the Wolverine began life as the Seeandbee and the Sable was the Greater Buffalo. During World War II, with aircraft carriers and escort vessels in short supply, the navy converted the two ships so they could train flyers stationed at Glenview. Safe on Lake Michigan, the carriers needed no precious escort destroyers. After training a total of 14,595 flyers, the ships were decommissioned and sold for scrap at war's end. The 550-foot baby flat tops were not, however, the largest ships ever to sail the lake. Steel firms have ships one and a half to twice that long.

"How are Chicago's water cribs anchored to the bottom of the lake? Does the foundation run all the way to the lake floor, or is there some other method used? If there is a foundation, did the engineers use sand or stone fill?"
—L. Ruth Cline

The water cribs are nothing more than protection walls for intake pipes leading to the 16-foot high tunnels nearly 200 feet beneath the lake floor which connect with the filtration plants. From above, the cribs look like huge donuts. In the well room or "hole," stands the intake pipe, covered by screens which are cleaned constantly by the crew. The city's newest crib was named after Mayor William E. Dever and stands next to the Carter Harrison crib about 2 miles off North Avenue. On July 25,1928, it was towed into the lake and sunk in its present position. Afterward, the space between its two steel casings was filled with concrete. Older cribs were weighted with stone. Each week, a shore boat brings out supplies and a 4-man relief crew, then leaves the men to 7 days of peace and quiet.

"How much water can Chicago's two filtration plants handle a day? I'd be curious to know how they stack up with the 10 largest plants in the world."
—Stephen Adam, Cicero

Chicago's Department of Water and Sewers operates the world's two largest filtration plants. The central plant, 1000 E. Ohio St., has a rated capacity of 960 million gallons a day and a peak capability of one billion, 700 million gallons a day. Its counterpart at 3300 E. Cheltenham Pl., has a rated capacity of 480 million gallons, with a peak capacity of 850 millions. The Bureau of Water is sending you a brochure which describes the Chicago water system and is including the total and average pumpages from 1965-69 for the two plants. Write the American Water Works Association, Inc., 2 Park Ave., New York, N. Y. 10016, for information on other domestic and foreign filtration plants.

"Chicago always had a submarine docked at the Naval Armory where visitors could take tours. Someone told me this is no longer possible. What happened?"—H.W.

Government cutbacks in the Naval reserve program rendered the Silversides expendable as a training craft for reservists. The Navy had planned on scrapping the submarine, but several groups took up the rallying cry of "Save the Silverside" as a memorial. The Combined Great Lakes Navy Association eventually was awarded the sub. Headed by Thomas J. Carroll, the group plans on restoring the Silversides as a display item. Carroll, owner of the River's End Marina Inc. here in Chicago, claims the process will take about two years, and the organization will begin a fund drive to accomplish this. Just where the submarine will rest is impossible to say, said Carroll, since two years is a long way off. The Silversides, by the way, was part of the Pacific fleet in World War II and is credited with sinking 29 ships and with having the second largest tonnage of any ship during the war.

"My 12-year old daughter has been bugging me to take her fishing in Lake Michigan. Reluctantly, I agreed to at least find out whether we need licenses, and where we can get them. Also, does the lake have anything besides alewives and coho salmon?"—P.G., Des Plaines

Here's your chance to show off. Inform your daughter that Lake Michigan has more than 200 species and subspecies of fish in its waters. Yellow perch is the most common and probably the most popular. And you do need a license to fish in Lake Michigan, but your daughter, since she is under 16, doesn't need to be licensed. You can get yours by writing to the Illinois Department of Conservation, 1227 S. Michigan Ave., Chicago or going to a bait and tackle shop along the lake. Persons over 65 or disabled veterans have to pay only 50 cents.

Monuments and Memorials

"Hope you won't think I'm stupid for asking this question, but I'm new to Chicago. Someone told me there is a statue of Grant in Lincoln Park as well as a statue of Lincoln in Grant Park. Is this really so?"—Trudy Zelinski

Yes, Trudy, there is a statue of Grant in Lincoln Park and a statue of Lincoln in Grant Park. To confuse you further, there is a statue of Honest Abe in Lincoln Park, but alas, there isn't one of Ulysses in Grant Park.

"In a recent paper, I noticed a picture of an employee cleaning the interior of Chicago's Water Tower at Chicago and Michigan Avenues. Does the Water Tower have any function other than historical?"
—*Charles Coil, Niles*

Chicago's most famous monument is not used except as a landmark. But what a history it has had! The cornerstone was laid in 1867, and the work finished in 1869. In 1871, it withstood the main thrust of the Chicago Fire and has been considered since a memorial to the estimated 300 killed in the disaster. Its day-to-day task was to camouflage a 138-foot-high standpipe used to even out the fluctuations in water pressure from Old Dally, the water pump for the North Side. The pump was removed in 1904 and the Water Tower became useless. Since then, it has withstood demolition campaigns, the widening of Michigan Avenue, and the rumor of leprechauns in its parapets. The station on the east side of Michigan, however, is still used and has a pumping capacity of 260 million gallons a day.

"I understand that Lincoln Park used to be a cemetery. Could you tell me why the mausoleum for someone named Couch was left standing?"
—Randie Rimmel

In 1865, when the graves were moved, the Couch family carried its protest to the courts. A United States Supreme Court decision at the time declared graves belong to the dead and not the living. That, plus the fact the family owned full deed to the property, helped win the case. The mausoleum originally was built for 11 and estimates as to the number of persons entombed in it, according to the Chicago Historical Society, vary from 1 to 13. One sure occupant is Ira Couch, who died in 1852 and who helped build the Tremont House, an early Chicago hotel.

"Did Chicago have its own King Tut? I couldn't believe my eyes. I was riding a north-south 'L' when it passed Irving Park Road. There in the middle of a cemetery was a pyramid. It was by no means as large as the famous ones in Egypt, but it obviously was serving the same purpose as they did. Who was the pharaoh it was built for and what's its story?"
—K.L. Himes

The cemetery you were passing is Graceland, one full of man's unique monuments to himself. The pyramid mausoleum was built for Peter Schoenhofen around the turn of the century. He was one of the city's most prominent brewmasters and a millionaire. His family always retained its ties with Peter's native Germany, and the family's property was seized during World War I. A descendant of Peter, Graf Schenk, was the man who carried the portfolio with a bomb into Hitler's meeting room in the unsuccessful attempt on his life.

"People have told me about a grave marker in Graceland Cemetery which is in the form of a baseball. Could you tell me something about it?"—J.G.

The monument stands over the grave of William A. Hulbert, the man who founded the National League. Carved on the marker are the names of the first N.L. franchise cities—Chicago, Cincinnati, Louisville, St. Louis, Boston, Hartford, Brooklyn, Philadelphia, Providence, Worcester, Cleveland and Detroit. Hulbert got into baseball in 1875 by becoming president of the Chicago ball club, which later evolved into the Chicago Cubs. Being somewhat of a newcomer to the sport, Hulbert refused to go along with an unwritten law among the owners not to raid the rosters of other clubs, as players were then signing only one-year contracts without any reserve clauses. Hulbert prepared for the 1876 season by signing Boston's "Big Four," pitcher Al Spaulding, catchers Cal McVey and James (Deacon) White, and second baseman Ross Barnes. Hulbert then got the support of the other owners in organizing the league, complete with constitution and standard player contracts. Hulbert nominated Morgan Bulkeley as its first president and succeeded him when he died a year later.

"A number of people in South Shore claim that the gilded statue of Columbia in Jackson Park is rotated every two or three years to face east and then west. Is this true?"
—A. Gunport

This is easily the most far-fetched question to come along in a while. Ironically, your question does have some slight basis in fact. The "Golden Lady" stands facing eastward today, on the site of the Columbian Exposition's administration building. Back in 1893, she stood at the other end of the lagoon in front of the administration building facing west. However, since "Maggie Murphy," as the park district boys affectionately call her, weighs over 100 tons, they haven't bothered to swivel her around on her pedestal in the last 70-odd years.

"Could you check out the name of the sculptor who did the extremely attractive statue in the little triangle park at the corner of Clark Street and Belden Avenue? I've heard that it is a Lorado Taft piece and was found in a warehouse."
—*Theresa Loftus*

You heard correctly. The piece was completed in 1914 as part of a bandstand in Lincoln Park. The stand was torn down in 1939, however, and stored in the Park District's service yard. It was discovered there and made the center of the park the city put together in 1969. The statue was done by Chicago's most famous sculptor, Lorado Taft, but left unnamed. It is often referred to simply as "the seated woman." When it was placed in the little park, there was talk of a plaque to inform people about the statue, but city planner Steve Roman says, "It hasn't proved necessary. The park was conceived of as a conversation plaza and has been so successful that everyone tells anyone new all about the statue."

"Can you plan an interesting day next week for my husband, myself and our two children to celebrate our 25th wedding anniversary? We cannot afford a big party, so it will be just the four of us. We would like to spend a memorable day- one the children will remember and so will we."—Mrs. S.S.

Try this tour recommended by the Chicago Convention and Tourism Bureau to visiting newsmen and foreign dignitaries. Drive to the Chicago Police Headquarters, 1121 S. State Street, and take the self-guided tour. Then go to the Fire Academy at 550 W. De Koven St. Then to the ultramodern University of Illinois Circle Campus at Taylor and Halsted Streets and visit the magnificently restored Hull House on campus. Then go to 22nd Street and Wentworth Avenue, Chicago's Chinatown, and then south on King Drive to Washington Park, site of Lorado Taft's world-famous Fountain of Time. Continue south to 57th Street and turn east through the University of Chicago campus and north on Ellis Avenue, passing Henry Moore's sculpture at the site of the first sustained nuclear reaction. Then go to Harper Court, a quaint new shopping center with interesting shops and eating places. Return via the Museum of Science and Industry, 57th Street and South Shore Drive, the Field Museum, Planetarium and Astronomical Museum and the Art Institute.

"For many years, I have passed the Woodlawn Cemetery in Forest Park and noticed several statues of elephants there. This is the first time that I have seen animals in a cemetery where humans are buried. What is the story behind them?"
—Charles F. Donald, Elmhurst

The five elephants stand as a memorial to the 68 members of a circus who were killed in a train wreck near Hammond, Ind., in 1918. They were erected by the Showmen's League of America to mark the plot where 53 of the victims are buried. The legend that the circus elephants helped to rescue the injured and are also buried in the plot is not true.

"Looking through a telescope from the Prudential building toward the south and slightly west, I saw a statue on top of some building. What was it?"
—Mrs. G.

Ceres, the six-ton lady who stands 31 feet 6 inches high on the Board of Trade building at Jackson and LaSalle. She's 45 stories, or 525 feet, above the street. Ceres is the goddess of grain.

"We are planning a trip to Chicago in the spring as sort of a second honeymoon trip. We figure on taking in most of the usual sights, but I wonder whether my wife (she's never been to your town) will have an opportunity to see Buckingham Fountain in operation. When is the water turned on?"
—J.S., Springfield, Ill.

Water is turned on by the Chicago Park District on May 20 every year. While your wife is watching, surprise her with a few facts and statistics: Clarence Buckingham Fountain was completed in 1927 at a cost of nearly $750,000, being donated to the city by Kate Sturges Buckingham, a patron of the arts, as a memorial to her brother. The main jet shoots 135 feet into the air and is surrounded by 133 lesser jets which use more than 15,000 gallons of water a minute. Park District officials claim the fountain is the largest and most beautiful in the world. Miss Buckingham left a trust fund to pay for its perpetual maintenance, which costs about $14,000 a year. The fountain is on from 11:30 a.m. to 3 p.m. and from 5 to 10 p.m., with the colors on during the last hour.

"Can you tell me if there is a statue of Gen. John Alexander Logan in Chicago? In a recent letter from my grandmother in downstate Illinois, she mentioned being one of his descendants. She has asked if I'd find her a picture of this monument."
—Mrs. Wadena Gerardi, Chicago Heights

The statue of John A. (Black Jack) Logan stands at 9th Street and Michigan Avenue. Executed by the famed Augustus Saint-Gaudens, it was unveiled in 1897. Logan was neither a professional soldier nor a graduate of West Point, but he was credited with saving the federal troops from sure defeat in Gen. Sherman's famous Atlanta campaign. When James B. McPherson was killed, Logan took command and turned defeat into victory. Yet, Logan was denied permanent command of the Army of the Tennessee because of what he said was discrimination due to West Point prejudice against volunteers. Logan, however, is probably more famous for founding a holiday—Memorial Day. When the Civil War was over, he became commander of the Grand Army of the Republic. On May 5, 1868, he issued an order designating the following May 30 as a memorial to dead comrades. Logan died a senator on Dec. 26, 1886, after an unsuccessful attempt to become Vice President.

"Is there any place in Chicago, preferably on the North Side, where I can go to play chess? I'm 16 and I just love the game."
—*Chess Player*

For a person with your hobby, Chicago certainly is the place to live. The Chicago Chess Club (founded in 1870) is open every afternoon and evening at its 64 E. Van Buren St. location. Membership for juniors is $15. On Friday evenings, in your own neighborhood, you can go to the Gompers Park Chess Club at 4222 Foster Ave. And, any time of the day or night (up to 11 p.m.) you can play chess in one of the most unique settings in the world, the Chess Pavilion at North Avenue Beach. The site overlooks downtown, Lake Michigan, and is a popular part of the beach for bikinis.

"My children and I are very curious about a statue in Graceland Cemetery at Irving Park Road and Clark Street. One can hardly miss the monument because of its vivid green color and its height of 12 to 15 feet. It represents a hooded figure with an arm across the lower part of the face. We want to know the name of the statue and its author."—Mrs. Laura Warner

The statue was done by the famous sculptor, Lorado Taft. It was cast in bronze and the green color is the result of natural corrosion. The background is polished granite. The name of the piece is "Death" and it stands on the plot of an early Chicago pioneer family by the name of "Graves."

"I have passed the Baha'i Temple in Wilmette many times and we have a family discussion going about it. Is Baha'i an Indian or Middle East religion? And why was their church built here?"
—R. Diedrichs

The Baha'i faith is a world religion which originated in Persia. Its prophet-founder Baha'u'llah - whose name means the "Glory of God" - died in the Holy Land in 1892. Baha'i world membership is estimated at 2,000,000. The faith, according to a spokesman, stresses the oneness of God, the oneness of humanity, and the oneness of religion. There are several thousand members in the Chicago area. The beautiful temple was built here because of the desire of the faith's founder to have houses of worship around the world open to all for meditation and prayer. The hours are daily and Sunday from 10 a.m. to 9 p.m. Tours are available for groups by calling AL 6-1154.

"Action Line recently ran a picture of a mural at Irving Park and Sheridan Roads. As an art student, I see this as the coming wave. Could you tell where other outdoor murals have been painted in Chicago? I want to put together a slide story of them."
—Chester Bakis

The number of wall murals in Chicago certainly is on the rise. The pictures and their titles speak for themselves. The following is a list of some of the more prominent ones. "The Wall of Respect and Truth" at 43rd St. and Langley Ave. "The Wall of Choices," at Halsted and 18th St.
"All Power to the people" (St. Dominic's Church) at 357 W. Locust St., "The Wall of Understanding" at Orleans and Locust Sts., "The Unity of the People" at Madison and Pulaski Rd. and "The Black Man's Dilemma" at 3702 W. 16th St.
More are being added constantly.

Nostalgia

"To collect a bet my husband has to prove he saw Buffalo Bill Cody here in Chicago sometime between 1914 and 1917. Born in 1909, my spouse is certain of it because he recalls attending the cowboy's wild west show at White City when he was 6 or 7. Do you have any information? Also, what ever happened to that amusement park?"
—Marie Welke, Berwyn

William Frederick Cody brought his rootin'-tootin' wild west show to Chicago on a number of occasions and appeared at White City in July, 1915. Cody was with the show until 1916 and died Jan. 10, 1917, at the age of 71. White City Amusement Park at 63rd Street and South Park Way was quite an attraction when it opened in 1904 and contained something for everybody: Rides, funhouses, ballrooms, restaurants, band concerts, shows, and roller skating. In the evening, a gala display of fireworks dazzled crowds gazing from the outdoor beer garden, where a shy blonde, Sophie Tucker, made her debut. A fire in 1927 destroyed several buildings and the park never recovered. Business went into the red, and in 1933 it went into receivership. A business combine, using a new name of "City of Mars," failed to give it new life and White City finally was condemned as a fire hazard and razed in 1939.

"This question goes even beyond grandmother's age and memory. I've been trying to find out when Chicago got its first gas street lamps and when did they finally disappear?"—R.C., Homewood

Chicago got lit up in 1850. Our city, with population of 300,000, was considered still a frontier town. People probably cheered on Sept. 4 when 36 lamps flickered on in City Hall, and in the homes of 125 customers. Before then, sensitive noses tried hard to accustom themselves to the odor of burning whale oil and eyes to semidarkness in homes. Our first gas plant was operated by the Chicago Gas Light and Coke Co., and could make and store just 15,000 cubic feet of gas for a single night's use. Today, Peoples Gas, which eventually absorbed the original firm, turns out up to one billion 757 million cubic feet for one 24-hour period. Gas lamps outlasted their lamplighters when the burners were equipped with pilot lights and time clocks. But timers, like your watch, have a habit of running too fast, slow or even not at all. Finally in 1954, the last gas lamps were uprooted from Chicago's curbs. The nostalgic lights, however, refused to die and since 1963 they have been used to light Wells Street in Old Town - at the special expense of the merchants there.

"I claim the Graf Zeppelin II, the sister ship of the Hindenburg which burned at Lakehurst, N.J. in 1937, made a maiden voyage to America. The airship flew over Chicago and then landed at Glenview Airport to refuel. This happened in 1938, and the Germans were just able to get home before the war started. So help me, this really happened, but the old timers around here don't seem to remember this. Could you back me up?"
—Charles Brinkmeyer, Glenview

Your facts are a little scrambled, but you're right about the Graf Zeppelin being there. First of all, there was only one Graf Zeppelin, and she visited Chicago twice. The first occasion was in 1929 on her first round-the-world flight. That time she just cruised over the city and let the inhabitants gawk. The Nazis sent her back in 1933 for The Century of Progress with goodwill ambassador Dr. Hugo Eckener aboard. In the midst of the fog and rain on Oct. 26, the great airship landed at Curtis-Wright Reynolds airport, the forerunner of Glenview Naval Air Station. Held on the ground by 250 strong-armed soldiers from Camp Whistler, the dirigible stayed only 29 minutes - just enough to let Dr. Eckener get off. The Germans then made a pass over Chicago before heading back to Akron, but the fog was so heavy that only those along the lake could see the Graf Zeppelin.

"During the 1930s, my mother took me to the Coliseum to see the walkathons (not marathons). She was an avid fan and we spent many, many nights watching these shows. I particularly remember Ruthie Carroll Arnold setting the record for staying in ice the longest. Could you verify these facts for my friends."—V.K.B.

Chicago certainly did have its pathetic walkathons during the 1930s. Allan DuBois and Ann Garry, for example, each walked 3,466 miles in one to win $500 apiece. Ruthie Carroll did seal herself in ice as part of the program. Other contestants got married as part of the show, while some women participated in slugfests on a mud-covered surface. Nurses were used as props, but became necessary by the end as people drove themselves to exhaustion. In Missouri, the events were ruled illegal because the attorney general maintained that the women were merely employees and therefore subject to the state's maximum daily hour provisions for women and children.

"The newspapers said the Shriners' Parade was the biggest ever held in the world, but I seem to remember a much bigger one held in Chicago in the 1930s. Do you?"—E.B., Kenosha

Yes. Your memory is better than Shrine press agents and parade writers. In 1933, when the American Legion held its national convention here, 120,000 Legionaires marched down Michigan Avenue 16 abreast in a parade that was 20 miles long. The marchers, including 535 drum and bugle corps, stepped off at 10 a.m. and the last ones were still walking at dusk. Schools were closed so youngsters could go downtown and watch "the greatest parade Chicago ever witnessed." In 1939, the Legion returned to Chicago to hold another spectacular parade, lasting 12 hours.

"When I was a kid, I vaguely remember a batch of Italians landing with some seaplanes in Lake Michigan. Can you refresh my memory by telling me what this was all about?"—F.H.

Flamboyant Gen. Italo Balbo, on July 15, 1933, guided his squadron of 24 seaplanes to a landing off Navy Pier in conjunction with the Worlds Fair. Along with his 96 airmen, he was given a hero's welcome by more than one million Chicagoans. The city then named Balbo Drive after the 37-year-old aviator and erected a Roman column near Burnham Harbor to commemorate the flight. In those days, Balbo was Mussolini's top lieutenant but evidently grew too popular at home, because Il Duce later demoted him to air minister and exiled Balbo to Libya as governor. Two weeks after Italy entered World War II, Balbo's bomber mysteriously exploded over Tobruk, killing all aboard.

Take your tykes to the statue of Grant that is east of the boat pond and the farm in the zoo, and you can look down the daring course that you and other Chicago youngsters sped down in your grab for glory. The contest, co-sponsored by the Herald-American and the Chevrolet division of General Motors Corp., led to the finals in Akron. Cars took off from a wooden ramp and, in later years, a celebrity pulled a lever to release them. The course was steep, but nothing compared to the one in Gary, which in 1947 injured seven kids, putting four of them in the hospital.

167

"Could you get me some information about a large snow vehicle that was built here in Chicago during the 1930s for a polar expedition? I was only 9 or 10 years old at the time and remember seeing it go down the street when they were testing it. The machine looked big to me and the tires were huge. Most of all, I'd like to know whatever happened to it."
—*Peter Lucchini*

The snow cruiser, built in 1939 for an expedition led by Adm. Richard Byrd, is frozen fast in Antarctica, where it had to be abandoned. The thing ranks with Howard Hughes' wooden airplane as one of the colossal engineering flops of history. The monstrous vehicle got stuck in a viaduct in the south side, was marooned on a sand dune in Indiana, collided with a truck elsewhere in Indiana, hit a bridge and plunged into a creek in Ohio, broke down twice in New York and caused a record traffic jam in Massachusetts. Ten feet had to be lopped off the back so it would fit on the boat bound for the Antarctic. Difficulties, of course, were encountered in unloading it there and it demolished a ramp in the process.

"Dad has been saving his World War II air raid warden helmet for years. When I asked him what his duties had been, he thought about it for so long that I gave up and went to my room. Would your newspaper clips contain what I want to know?"—W.T., Westmont

In February, 1942, civil defense block captains were instructed to recommend four persons on their blocks for appointment as air raid wardens. These were given a 25-hour crash course to prepare them for their duties: Watch for lights during blackout and see that they are extinguished; direct all persons to shelters determined beforehand; report to the central control office fallen bombs, fires and any suspicious gas; administer first aid and assist victims from bombed buildings; set an example of coolness and efficiency during the emergency. Patriotic rallies were used to stimulate the drive for the city's goal of 60,000 wardens. In a mass induction, for example, Mayor Edward J. Kelly swore in 4,000 milkmen in one shot.

"I would like some information about the old Villa Venice in Northbrook. Can you find out a little of its history and maybe get me a picture of it?"
—Wanda Harris, Des Plaines

The Villa Venice originally was a nightclub and restaurant known as "The House That Jack Built." It was remodeled in 1924 by Albert Bouche at a cost of $100,000 and renamed the Villa Venice. Elaborate musical revues were presented each season and patrons were serenaded by strolling fiddlers. Outside, guests could ride up and down the Des Plaines River in gondolas - with singing gondoliers. In recent years, Villa Venice received considerable publicity as the site for syndicate gatherings, especially weddings. Since the 1920s, it was the target of frequent gambling raids by state and local police. The place burned to the ground in 1967. Neither Jack nor the syndicate has offered to rebuild it.

"I'm from Danville, and the last 'extra' newspaper I can remember was when John Dillinger was killed in the '30s. My husband, however, is positive that they had 'extras' during the war. Could you tell us when the last extra edition was published?"
—Mrs. O.M. High
Hobart, Indiana

Extra edition newspapers were a part of journalism through the early days of World War II. The last one the Herald American printed was April 23, 1942, when Gen. Jimmy Doolittle raided Japan with his bombers. The "extra" was a method of getting important news to the public quickly in the days before radio was common. When a big story broke, battalions of newsboys were marshaled to snatch the papers as they came off the presses and hawk them in the streets. Today, with improved distribution techniques, the news story gets on the street faster than ever before through four regular editions and several replates. The only thing we lost was the newsboy running up and down the sidewalks yelling, "Extry! Extry! Read all about it!"

"Why did Jim Moran the Courtesy Man leave Chicago, and where is he now?"
—E.D. Sandwich, Ill.

Jim Moran pulled up stakes in 1968 because of his wife's health and to spend more time at their winter home in Pompano Beach, Fla. He was recently named president and chief executive officer of Southeast Toyota Distributors, Inc. Besides being involved in many philanthropic organizations here, Moran was quite a pioneer. He began his career by operating a gas station at Clark Street and Glenlake Avenue in 1939, building his business to a chain of three gas stations and a garage. Moran then purchased a Ford dealership in 1945, switching to Hudsons two years later. Fords reentered his life in 1956. He was the first auto dealer to sponsor a full feature program, and was the first dealer to offer used cars for sale on TV and sell them himself. Against the advice of others, Moran went ahead and sponsored movies on TV, sometimes cracking after one of his commercials: "O.K., you can come back in from the kitchen. Torture time is over." We masochists couldn't have been sadder when it really ended.

Streets

"Was Broadway ever called Evanston Avenue?"—H.H.

Broadway was known as Evanston Avenue until July 30, 1913. In the city's earlier years, when the area was Village of Lake View, various parts of the artery were also known as Plank Road, Clarendon Avenue, Lake Shore Avenue, and Dummy Road. The latter name came from the dummy (locomotive drawn transit) line that extended from Diversey to Graceland (now Irving Park Road).

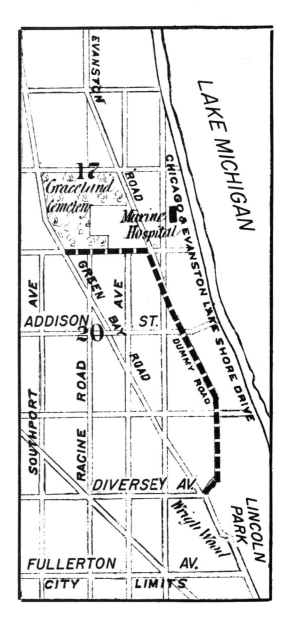

*"A long time ago, you
printed a question and
answer about Achsah
Bond Drive, which
connects Lake Shore
Drive with the
Planetarium. I tried to
remember who the
cause way was named
after in order to tell
some visitors and found
I had forgotten. I've
been trying to think of
the answer ever since.
Please help."*
—Richard Rollins,
Lincolnwood

Achsah Bond was the wife of Illinois' first governor. Her husband's name was a little unusual too; he was called Shadrach. He came to the Illinois country in 1794, obtaining a number of land grants, and became a prosperous farmer. When Illinois was admitted to the Union in 1818, he was elected our state's first governor, serving until 1822. Mrs. Bond was one of those hearty pioneer women without whom the wilderness never could have been settled. To honor her and the rest of the women of Illinois, the drive was dedicated on Illinois Day at the Century of Progress in 1933. At that time, the drive was little more than a flimsy bridge joining Northerly Island to the mainland. The ladies didn't let it stay that way long though, and it was widened and rebuilt to become a permanent causeway. A commemorative bronze plaque stands near the western approach.

"Have you ever seen that strange structure on Fullerton Avenue just west of Riis Park? It looks like a curved section of an elevated highway with no beginning or end. The structure stands on 40-foot pillars and there is no way to get a car up on it. What is it?"
—H.K.

It is what is left of a track for testing mobile radar equipment. When in use during World War II and the Korean War, the roadway continued to the ground. Mobile radar units were driven to the top of the structure which was then higher than any buildings on the far northwest side. Planes from Glenview flew over the area to test the accuracy of the radar. Western Electric, which manufactured the units, stopped using the facility after the Korean war.

177

"Is it true that Chicago was the scene of the world's first auto race? It seems like a strange place to hold such a contest."—Al Liber, Evanston

Thanksgiving day in 1895 marked the first automobile race in America—from Jackson Park to Evanston. Through 4 inches of snow, 6 machines, called "motorcycles" in those days, lurched away from the starting line near what is now the Museum of Science and Industry. Ten hours, 23 minutes later, Charles Duryea, piloting the car he built himself, crossed the finish line. The winning speed was a blazing 7 1/2 m. p. h. The only other car to finish was a Benz driven by H. Mueller of Decatur. The Chicago-Evanston race was the world's second — the first being from Paris to Bordeaux in June of the same year.

Black Chicago

"There is a statue at 35th Street and South Park Way which has been there for many years. What does it symbolize?"—Mrs. Ella Mitchell

The lower part of the monument is called "Victory" and is a tribute to the Black soldiers of the old Illinois National Guard 8th regiment who died during World War I. The unit, which was renamed the 370th infantry of the 93rd division, was in the thick of the fighting in the Somme and Argonne sectors. The monument was the work of sculptor Leonard Crunelle and was unveiled in 1927. The figure of the doughboy on top of the memorial was dedicated in 1936 to all the Black soldiers who died in the war.

"Right after the first World War, there was a race riot on the South Side that old-timers say was much more serious than any we have had since. However, the Chicago police were able to handle the trouble quickly and efficiently. How come they can't manage things as well today? Do you think it's because they have lowered the standards for candidates, and instead of demanding strength, common sense, and size, they now stress things like psychology, empathy, and brotherhood?"
—A.L.B.

The race riot, which raged in Chicago from July 27 to Aug. 3, 1919, was hardly handled "quickly." According to historians Herman Kogan and Lloyd Wendt, "Police were actually powerless to do much but stop sporadic fights." In the meantime, black and white mobs shot, stabbed, and stoned anyone of the opposite color who came in sight. Houses were set ablaze by cheering throngs as real guerrilla warfare convulsed the city. Finally, on July 30, 6,000 state troops were called in and finally restored order. The coroner set the cost of the riot in human lives lost at 38—15 white and 23 black. Worst hit was the area around the stockyards. Police were accused of shooting wildly into crowds at the time.

"I am doing some research on my aunt, Willa Brown, the aviatrix. I would like to know whether it is possible to get news clippings or pictures of her. Here's what I have: She was first a school teacher at Wendell Phillips High School. Then she went into aviation and had her own flying school in Chicago. She trained instructors who later became teachers at Tuskegee Institute to train the all-black 99th pursuit squadron in World War II. She once flew Eleanor Roosevelt. In 1948, she ran for Congress. I would appreciate any more information you can give me."
—*David Brown*

We're sending you clippings. You have quite an aunt. In 1938, at 32, she became the first black woman in the country to receive a private pilot's license. In 1948, she ran for Congress in the 1st district and, before that, had tried for alderman and Republican ward committeeman. In 1949, she sought unsuccessfully federal funds for a black-operated airport in Chicago area, because of the lack of openings for blacks in the airline industry in Chicago. We hear she married the pastor of the West Side Community Church and is still teaching aeronautics.

"We are working with a group of black students this summer, tutoring them and taking them to various places around the city. We are looking for something to do together that will help their appreciation of Negro history as well as our own."—E.L., Wheaton

The Museum of African-American History at 3806 Michigan Ave., is made to order for you. It offers a room of African artifacts as well as relics and documents from Negro American history. Included are mementos of the famed Hudlun family, known as the "angels of the Chicago fire." The black community, we are informed, was left untouched by the disaster and the Hudluns were foremost among those who spent themselves administering to its victims. The museum is open from 12:30 p.m. to 4:30 p.m. every day except holidays.

"I was quite astonished when a friend told me about a race riot here in Cicero in 1951, the year I was born. Did this actually happen?"
—Thomas Martin, Cicero

It did. Henry Clark Jr., then a 29-year-old black bus driver, got an apartment through a real estate concern. He, his wife and children thought the apartment was in Chicago. An angry, shouting mob was the welcome. Guarded by police and deputy sheriffs ordered by the United States District Court, the Clarks courageously moved in the building at 6139 W. 19th St. on July 10, amid jeers and taunts. The mob broke into the apartment that night, wrecked everything and hurled torches into the structure. The crowd, which numbered 3,000 at one time, fought police and deputies. Gov. Adlai Stevenson had to call out five companies of National Guardsmen. Three policemen and nine civilians were hospitalized.

"I have a question concerning Jesse Jackson of Operation PUSH. Is he really an ordained minister and entitled to use the 'Reverend' before his name or did he just assume that title?"
—Louie Martin

The Rev. Jesse Jackson is an ordained minister in the Baptist Church. He attended the Chicago Theological Seminary after graduation from North Carolina Agricultural and Technical College in Greensboro, N. C. He was star quarterback and student body president. He is married and has three children. His civil rights leadership dates back to his college days when he led sit-ins at hotels, motels, theaters and lunch counters in Greensboro in 1963.

Firefighters and Cops

"Could you find out for me about a police sergeant, Harry Kellogg. He supposedly shot and killed a judge who had held him in contempt of court back in 1916 or 1917."—James Leary

Harry Kellogg, known as Chicago's "millionaire policeman," led a multiple life prior to the courtroom fireworks in July, 1921. Besides being a lawman, Kellogg was reputed to be a bootlegger, dive-keeper, money lender and real estate shark. His appearance in court was due to a legal squabble involving 15 acres of Arlington Heights land, which he refused to vacate, ignoring two previous court orders. When Judge Charles A. McDonald sentenced Kellogg to a $100 fine and 15 days in jail, the policeman mumbled something about "persecution," whipped out his police revolver and began shooting. Two bullets hit Attorney Lemuel M. Ackley, who died in a hospital, while another bullet clipped the bench two feet away from the judge's face. Kellogg then aimed his gun at his own head, missed twice, sending the crowd of spectators stampeding for the doors. The sixth bullet, however, found its mark. Kellogg recuperated, but while awaiting trial on murder charges in the County Jail, he committed suicide by taking potassium cyanide which had been smuggled in.

"I remember, as a boy, Chicago's horse-drawn fire and police wagons. When were they last used? Could I get a picture of either as a memento?"—Steve Lacoco

Nostalgia, that's the name of the malady which infects old timers when we recall those old days. Buck and Beauty were the horses which pulled Engineer John Kelly, Driver Jim O'Leary and Fireman J. Maher on Engine No. 11 in response to Box 848 at Chicago Avenue and State Street at 12:40 p.m. on Feb. 5, 1923. The equipment never returned to its quarters because, in its absence, a new gasoline-driven pumper replaced it. The first gasoline-driven fire equipment was put in service in 1912. The police records are not so distinctive because they were progressing faster in a vain effort to keep up with the hoodlum element spawned by the Volstead Act (Prohibition) of 1919. The police, of course, could use the 'speedy' autos then available whereas firemen had to wait for the better development of trucks for their heavier and more specialized equipment. There was pollution then, too, with special clean-up squads trailing old dobbin down the cobble-brick streets. But that pollution was good for the grass.

"Why is a paddy wagon called a paddy wagon?"—K. R.

Because of an old ditty:

"Paddy, get the wagon,
We have an old souse here;
We'll haul him to the station
Because he's full of beer."

"Paddy," according to the story, was a police officer who was toting a drunk down west Madison Street in 1878. He was finding the trip to the police station, as usual, laborious. A merchant by the name of Frank Claussen told him, "Toss him in the wagon, Pat, and I'll drive him to the station for you." The merchant did and repeated the job on a number of future occasions, for which he was reimbursed. The police department took up the idea and bought their own wagons later that year.

"Weren't the lights in traffic signals once just the opposite of the way they are now? I'm having trouble convincing a friend that once the yellow was on top, green was in the middle and red was on the bottom."—R. Mays

Right you are. When Chicago's first traffic signal went on duty, the lights were positioned as you say. Called a "dummy policeman," it was installed on Oct. 29, 1921 at Jackson Boulevard and Ashland Avenue while other cities relied on hand-operated devices. Motorists were probably grinding tooth and gear when the West Chicago Park commissioners, the forerunner of the Park District, issued a subsequent report and stated". . . another innovation to aid the motorists is the automatic signal tower which flashes Go and Stop." The lights were later standardized as we know them in the 1940s.

YELLOW-TRAFFIC CHANGE
GREEN-GO
RED-STOP

Chicago's Amusements

"This is going back a few years, but I wonder what happened to the buildings from the Columbian Exposition of 1893. I have souvenirs from when it was held in Jackson Park and would like to know."—B.I., Riverside

What a history those buildings had! The Fine Arts Building, of course, was reconstructed and now houses the Museum of Science and Industry. The Court of Honor was destroyed by fire when the fair was coming to a close. It consisted of the Mines and Mining Building, Electricity Building, Manufacturers and Liberal Arts Building, Machinery Hall and the Agricultural Building. The Cold Storage Building, which helped introduce the manufacture of ice to the world, burned on July 10, 1893, killing four firemen and eight employees. A fur trapper bought the Delaware Building and had it reconstructed along the shore of Wolf Lake on private property (someone else's). The Wrigley family bought the Norway Building for its Lake Geneva estate, just as Frank Chandler did with the Ceylon Court, a Singhalese temple. The original structure of La Rabida sanitarium in Jackson Park was the Spanish Building for the fair, but was long ago torn down.

"I'm told the first ferris wheel was operated here in Chicago. Do you have any facts among your clips to substantiate this, and who invented it?"
—W.W.

George W. Ferris invented his wheel in 1892 at a supposed cost of $300,000. Chicagoans were then experiencing a depression, and his project was considered pure folly. Ferris went ahead, however, and constructed the wheel for the World Columbian Exposition of 1893. He was at first denied concession rights, but it was eventually erected after the opening of the exposition. The original wheel, by the way, could carry 2,160 passengers in its 36 cars.

"Every time I hear futuristic plans for the Loop, people talk about moving sidewalks. Your item on the Columbian Exposition of 1893 reminded me that I had heard they were used then. What ever happened?"
—J. Christiansen

Early plans for the Columbian Exposition called for moving sidewalks throughout the fair area. The same objection, however, arose which has ever since. What about people in wheel chairs or with canes? The whole system was finally exiled to a pier that extended 2,500 feet into Lake Michigan. On that limited basis, the moving sidewalks proved highly successful. Chairs were attached to the sidewalks and it was entirely sheltered. People often sat down, took their shoes off and went to sleep for a few hours.

"When I was a kid, I used to jump on my bike and pedal over to the yacht harbor in Jackson Park and sit for hours looking at the replica of the Santa Maria. My favorite boyhood fantasy was to rebuild the ship and go adventuring in her, usually as a pirate. I've been away from the city for many years and I see that Jackson Park isn't the same any more. Even the Santa Maria is gone. Could you tell me what happened to her?"
—Fred Ransome

The Santa Maria, the Pinta and the Nina were sent to the Columbian Exposition of 1893 as a gift of the Spanish government. The replicas of Columbus' three caravels were the hit of the exposition and thousands of visitors trooped aboard. When the fair closed, the vessels were turned over to the South Park District. In spite of ambitious plans to save the ships the Pinta was dismantled in 1918, and the Nina was destroyed by fire a year later. The Santa Maria took part in a festival at Municipal (now Navy) Pier in 1921 and then was towed back to Jackson Park, where she peacefully rotted away. In 1952, she was broken up by a wrecking firm.

"We would like to find out something about the history of Riverview park so we can have some peace in our family. My husband says it originally was a circus or carnival, but this doesn't seem right to me. Also, could you find out if the parachute ride used to be a sightseeing tower for the World's fair in 1933? My grandmother seems sure of this, although she can't remember when Riverview started, and she is in her 70s. Thanks and GOOD LUCK."
—Mrs. Mary Cihlar, Norridge

Riverview was the brainchild of William Schmidt,who set up shop in 1904 on the old rifle range of the German Sharpshooters club at Western and Belmont Avenues. A water slide, merry-go-round, goat cart rides, and a shooting gallery were the main attractions, along with a beer garden and bandstand where John Philip Sousa once played. The parachutes came along in 1936 when Schmidt's son, George, converted a 220-foot sightseeing tower for the job. The tower, which originally had elevators instead of parachutes, was built in 1908. That was the year the hand-carved merry-go-round horses arrived from Europe. Those horses were sold when Riverview closed and are still carrying children in another amusement park.

"I'm starting a little project that requires some historical information on Navy Pier. How can I get my hands on some?"
—Richard Herr

Booklets and brochures are coming, courtesy of the Department of the Port of Chicago. Here's more: Originally known as Municipal Pier at its opening in 1916, it was designed to be the pleasure playground of the city. Cooled by lake breezes, Municipal Pier offered dining, drinking and dancing for work-weary Chicagoans in the pre-air conditioner era. Sightseeing boats left wakes from the pier to Lincoln and Jackson Parks, while crowds sipped beer, listening to wind-carried music that wafted from the huge auditorium-ballroom at the pier's eastern edge, the end of the line for the Grand Avenue street car. After World War I, the structure was renamed in honor of the Navy dead. The lavish balls that were held there couldn't keep Navy Pier financially above water, and revenue was hindered by prohibition and later depression. During World War II, however, things perked up and the pier found employment as a Navy training station; later, it housed the Chicago Campus of the University of Illinois. Today, the pier is being useful again as a cargo terminal for lake shipping. But its glory days seem gone forever.

"A buddy of mine recently was recalling his Riverview Park days. During the conversation, the subject of the park's famous roller coaster, the Bobs, came up. When we talked of speed, we were miles apart. Just how fast was this ride, and was it the fastest in the world?"
—J.P., Deerfield

Officially, we'd have to agree with our clips, which say the Bobs attained speeds of 60 m.p.h. when plummeting downward and was one of the fastest roller coasters in the world. The current champ is the Bobs in Belle Vue Amusement Park in Manchester, England, which reaches speeds of 61 m.p.h. Operators of other famous roller coasters, however, are reluctant to disclose the speeds they attain.

Museum officials had to ponder over that question, since the uniqueness of many items make such evaluations almost impossible. No telling how much a German submarine or a coal mine might fetch. However, they believed that Colleen Moore's fairy castle doll house would have to be one of the most expensive items—valued in excess of $500,000. The former silent screen star started the project early in life when her father, an architect, said, "Let's build a doll house." It took nine years to complete and 700 artists and craftsmen contributed. Colleen Moore used her diamonds and pearls, for example, to make a chandelier, and she later traveled around the world collecting miniature treasures. The medieval, gothic castle that embraces all fairy tales toured America and people paid to see it. Proceeds were given to aid crippled children. Finally, the museum's president talked her into displaying the structure so all children could see the mechanical wonders and riches inside.

"For a biology project, I need information on the giant panda. Can you steer me to a few places I can write to obtain some literature?"
—Chris Tokarz

The Chicago Public Library, for starters, has a book for you, "The World of the Giant Panda" by Richard Perry, in the Natural Sciences and Useful Arts Department. You're also getting the names and addresses of a few other sources to write. Panda mania started in 1869, when Pere David officially discovered the creature for the western world. For decades after, the panda was the dream of every trophy hunter and all the animals that entered this country were very much dead. In 1934, however, William Harvest Harkness Jr. left New York with his new bride, determined to bring back a live panda. His expedition collapsed, and he died of a mysterious illness in February, 1936, stranded in Shanghai. Harkness' wife, Ruth, a tenderfoot dress designer, took up her husband's unfulfilled dream the following April. Following a 1,500-mile trip up the Yangtze, she endured a 300-mile trek with opium-addicted porters and periodic wheel barrow rides. She found the 10-day old, 3-pound Su-Lin in a tree and brought him home alive and to Brookfield. Unfortunately, Su-Lin died the next year.

"You ran an item about the most valuable possession in the Museum of Science and Industry. I am much more interested in animals. Could you tell me what's the most expensive animal in Lincoln Park Zoo? Also, what's second and third?"
—Richard Variani

In a way, it was as though we were asking Lincoln Park Zoo Director Dr. Lester Fisher which of his children he valued most. Nevertheless, he did try to be objective and put Sinbad the Gorilla at the top of the list. He said the zoo wouldn't take $50,000 for him. There was no way they'd sell him. Judy, the elephant, would also have been untouchable he said posthumously of the beloved pachyderm. In cash value, the rare snow leopards rate very high at $4,000 or $5,000 each. Mike, the polar bear, is valuable beyond the possibility of ever being sold, although a polar bear can be purchased for a mere $1,500.

*"Where can I get a
picture of Bushman? I
need it for Christmas."*
—D.P. Cesario

For Christmas? You must have found that one person who has everything. We are sending you a photo to give him or her. If you want to shop for your relatives, however, we suggest you visit the Field Museum of Natural History, where you can get all the picture postcards of Bushman you want. We'll even help you along with a little biography of Lincoln Park Zoo's famous gorilla. He weighed 550 pounds and stretched 6 feet, 2 inches. He was by no means the largest ever in captivity. That honor belongs to Mbongo, who weighed in at around 670 at the San Diego Zoo, before his death in 1942. It was just that Bushman was about the meanest. He died in 1950 and is now preserved in the Field Museum.

"Could you help me with a Christmas holiday suggestion? I'm going to be visiting Chicago with my two daughters, Marjie and Becky, who are in grade school. We'd like to do something special on this trip in connection with the holidays that will make the trip memorable."
—*Mary Lou Taylor, Silver Spring, Md.*

One very good suggestion coming up: Visit the Adler Planetarium. They have a special program, "The Star of Bethlehem," in which they recreate on the domed ceiling the sky as it was in the years around the birth of Christ. They explore the possibilities of what the star of Bethlehem might have been: a meteor, a new star or a conjunction of planets. All such manifestations were referred to as stars in those days. Shows begin at 11 a.m., 12:30 p.m. and 3:30 p.m. The planetarium is closed on Christmas and New Year's Day.

"Mom tells me that Judy, Lincoln Park Zoo's now deceased elephant, once walked all the way from Brookfield Zoo. She couldn't recall when it happened or why. Fill me in."—Mark, Brookfield

Judy was Brookfield Zoo's first elephant. Sold to the Chicago Park District for $2,500, the young lady of 25 years was to be transported to Chicago by truck. But on July 2, 1943, she refused to enter the van. Twenty zoo workers tried to pull her in with little success. Finally, in desperation, the Lincoln Park director snorted: "I'll fix her. Let her walk." The 18-mile trek took Judy 7 1/2 hours. Attendants shooed away her enemies, dogs and bicycles. Once in her new quarters, Judy, who had weighed 9,000 pounds, settled down to gain back the 224 pounds she had lost during the march. Judy was 65 when she died on March 23, 1971.

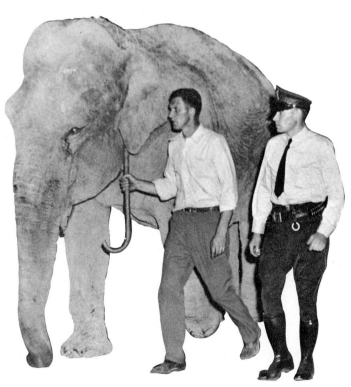

"Please settle a bet. Are elephants afraid of mice or not? I have a bet with my big brother that there isn't any animal they are afraid of."
—Jenny Holgren

Jenny, you simply have to learn how to bet. According to Dr. Joel Wallach, veterinarian at Brookfield Zoo, elephants are not afraid of mice. However, you lose your bet because he adds that, even in the wild, they fear man, and if they pick up a man's scent they'll run, rather than give chase. Several years ago spectators witnessed a mouse test Brookfield's rogue elephant Ziggy. The poor little rodent merely wanted to nibble on an apple core that had been thrown into Ziggy's pen. The mighty elephant watched the little creature - the only living thing to dare enter his domain in years. With a hurricane blast Ziggy sent the mouse flying into the next cage - disproving all those animated cartoons kids have been watching for years.

What a Town!

"Could you show me where I could get a map of the Loop showing how to avoid the cold and other discomforts by transferring through and under public buildings and stores?"
—S. Korzen

Few Chicagoans realize it, but they can enter and leave the Loop (on a subway) and travel from Marshall Field & Company to the Civic Center, then back under the Brunswick Building to Stevens or Wieboldt's without finding out what the weather is like. Along the concourses, they can find restaurants and a number of imaginative little stores. In addition, of course, a person can enter almost every major store along State Street directly from the subway. A less-attractive sheltered path also exists under both Wacker Drive and part of Michigan Avenue. Underground pathways, city planners assure us, represent the Loop of the future, as tunnels will connect every principal store and building downtown.
The most famous tunnel in the Loop is not even for people. It is a ten foot wide cow path that has been a legal right-of-way for the animals since 1833.

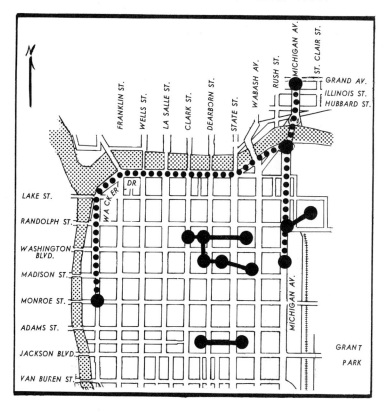

"I was married in the mouth of a whale exhibited here in Chicago in 1930 but my grandchildren won't believe me. I lost the pictures of the wedding. Can you find any newspaper pictures of the couples who were married in the mouth of that whale?"
—*Mrs. Emily (Baumann) Knurek*

Note to Mrs. Knurek's grandchildren: Those are your grandparents, over 40 years younger, in the rear. The couple on the left are Arley Anderson and Margaret Kennedy. The picture's caption at the time read: "Like Jonah, man of misfortune, who entered upon a long sea journey through the mouth of a whale, two couples last night began a life-long voyage on the sea of matrimony in the mouth of the great finback whale on exhibition."

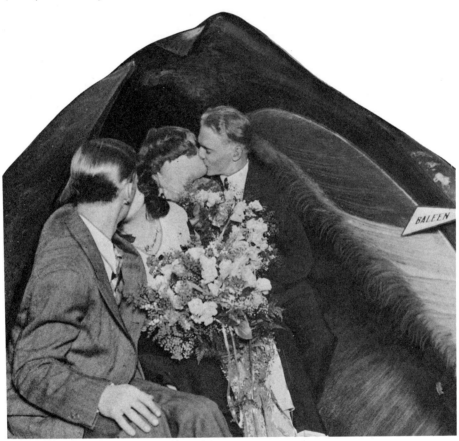

"My little brother has the biggest appetite I've ever seen. My boy friend and I took him to a drive-in hamburger place and he ordered 10 of them and gobbled them up. My friend had to pay the bill and he won't speak to me any more. I'm out a boyfriend, but my older brother thinks we may have gained a record breaker. Did he set some kind of mark?"
—D.D.

Your little brother has nothing on Phillip Yazdzik, a former Pennsylvania coal miner, who set a world's record here in Chicago in 1955 by downing 77 hamburgers, chased by 24 glasses of milk and 6 bottles of pop. Yazdzik shrugged it off as a mere "snack" and could have eaten more if the photographers hadn't made him nervous. Your brother is a growing boy and should do better when he gets older.

"Can you prove me right after all these years? I remember, when I was a little boy, that there was a flying machine at Chute's Park which was the marvel of the age. It had wings which flapped up and down. This was before the Wright brothers flew at Kitty Hawk, so you know it was a long time ago. Everybody thinks I'm crazy and I need you to back me up."—Eli Warren

It was a toughie, but we made it. The first problem was to find Chute's Park, which we learned was at Kedzie Avenue and Jackson Boulevard at the turn of the century. There, in 1902, a six-passenger dirigible with articulated wings appeared on the scene. Its inventor cranked up the engine and hopped aboard for a trial spin. The machine flapped madly, lurched a few feet into the air and collapsed in a heap of broken wood and torn fabric. No history was made that day.

The tunnels, 40 feet below ground level, span the area from Chicago Avenue to 16th Street and from Halsted Street to Wabash Avenue. Started in 1909, the Chicago Tunnel Co. was a flourishing business, supplying the buildings with coal and removing ashes, cinders and rubbish. Through 6-by-7-foot concrete horseshoe tubs ran 47 miles of 2-foot-gauge track on which 150 electric locomotives pulled 3,304 cars. The change from coal to oil put the system out of business. Today the passages sit unused, and the city is always looking for suggestions on what to do with them. Ideas have ranged from housing prisoners to starting a booming mushroom business in the almost constant 50-degree temperature and moist, dark conditions.

"Here's one to stir the old-timers. Can you give me some information, maybe even a picture, on the grave that is located at 93rd Street and Ewing Avenue? It was quite an attraction years ago."—Harry Grace

Andreas Von Zirngibl, with one arm and the aid of the Supreme Court, continues to rest undisturbed smack dab in the center of South Chicago's industrial district. Zirngibl, once a soldier in Blucher's army, lost his arm fighting Napoleon prior to coming to the U.S. in 1854. Paying $160 in gold for 44 acres of real estate on the Calumet River, the German native stipulated in his will that he be buried on the site. He died a year later and his son complied with his request. In 1877, however, Zirngibl's grave was the object of legal hassles and the courts declared the property belonged to the Chicago Canal and Dock Company, but granted the heirs title to the grave and a path leading to it. True ownership of the tract was shrouded in mystery because the historic Chicago Fire had obliterated records. More litigation followed throughout the years, but Von Zirngibl's grave still is being attended by his descendants.

The Windy City's Weather

"Please find out for me where the local Polar Bear club meets. I know the club exists; I have seen pictures of people diving into water cluttered with ice floes. All I need to know is where and when."—Shirley Benson

Alas and alack, the Polar Bear club is a thing of the past in Chicago. These hearty souls gathered near the Edgewater Beach Hotel every New Year's day for a dip in the icy waters of Lake Michigan. They would stop shivering long enough to pose for photographers and proclaim that theirs was the greatest sport in the world. The club met from 1924 to 1940, then passed from the scene. However, you'll be glad to know that Milwaukee still has a group of die-hard Polar Bears.

"Quite a few years ago there was a newspaper article about a young woman who fainted in the snow in subzero temperatures. Although she was almost frozen, she recovered the next morning. What happened to her after that? I can't remember."—Mary Krzyzanowski

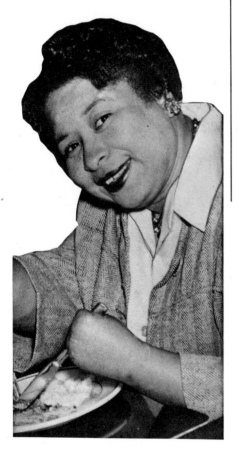

Mrs. Dorothy Mae Stevens, then 23, made medical history on Feb. 8, 1951. When she was found frozen in a South Side alley, her normal body temperature of 98.6 was down to a unprecedented low of 64 degrees. Her breathing was three to five times a minute. Normal is 18 to 22. Pulse was 12, compared to the usual 70 to 80 beats a minute. Even her blood pressure couldn't be recorded, since her blood had congealed to a sludge-like substance. Once in the hospital, she was given 200 milligrams of cortisone and blood plasma. The doctors who had saved her life, however, couldn't do the same for her limbs. A month later both legs had to be amputated nine inches below her knees and she eventually lost several fingers. Although the alcohol in her system was credited with saving her, she subsequently became involved in church work and in giving lectures on alcoholism.

"Will you put my smart-aleck son in his place? He claims that the big snow storm of January, 1967, could have come out only from the southwest. As I was the one who shoveled all day, I say it came out of the east. He insists that he's right; therefore we have this bet. Who wins?"—Mrs. Frank Murphy, Elmhurst

Your kid is right, but before the storm was over it had come at us from almost every direction. The National Weather Service says the center of the storm moved into our area from the southwest. Starting at 5:02 a.m. on Jan. 26, the storm finally ended at 3:05 p.m. on Jan. 27. Northeastern winds dominated the first day, backing into the north on the morning of the 27th. Winds then backed around from the northwest toward evening hours.

"Could you tell me what is the hottest day in the history of Chicago? Also, how hot does it have to be to fry an egg on the sidewalk? I remember seeing the picture of someone doing it in one of the papers about 15 years ago. Please answer as the temperature in our corner tavern gets hot enough without further arguments on these two questions."
—F. L.

The hottest day in the history of Chicago was July 24, 1934. The city sweltered in those pre-air conditioning days in 105 degrees. It need not get that warm, however, to do the egg-on-the-sidewalk bit. The picture we are printing was taken a number of years ago in an 87-degree temperature, but it can be even cooler, if the sun has heated the concrete sufficiently.

Only in Chicago

"This may sound crazy, but we would like to have our old car made into a coffee table. Our 1957 Chevy has served us faithfully, and rather than let it be ungraciously junked, we would like to keep it around the house. Is there any place in Chicago that could squash a 1957 Chevy into a nice neat bundle? And how much would it cost?"
—E. O. S.

For a mere $10, you can have old Nellie transformed into the heaviest coffee table in the neighborhood. Take the car to General Iron Industries, Inc., at 4600 Division St., and take along a truck to haul it away. A press will smash the old clunker into a package 5 feet long and 2 feet square. With the motor, it will then weigh about a ton and a half. We hope your living room floor can take the strain.

"Just recently, the last Navy ship here slipped moorings and sailed away, taking a great many memories. Will Chicago have a resident navy again?"
—Marguerite Conklin

No. The economy guillotine has again cut down tradition. The departure of the Parle, flagship of the "Corn Belt fleet," marked the end of that fleet and of an era which had seen United States naval ships on the Great Lakes since 1799. The ship had been used to train naval reservists during the summer months. None remain, and no return is planned. Other craft in the fleet were berthed in Detroit, Michigan City, Milwaukee, and Sheboygan. There are thousands of sailors still in the 9th naval district, most of them at Great Lakes.

"Just how many cruisers named 'Chicago' has the Navy had? My brother says there have been three, including the last one, a guided missile ship. However, it seems to me that there was another built during World War II with bonds bought by Chicagoans. That would bring the total up to four. Anyhow, settle this thing for us, will you?"
—Stefan Rodzak

There have only been three cruisers named Chicago. The first one combined sail and steam power and was commissioned in 1889. The second, a 10,000 ton "treaty cruiser" launched in 1930, was refurbished with the coming of World War II. She fought in the Pacific until 1943, when sunk by Japanese torpedo planes. The latest vessel to bear the name was launched in 1944, and reached the Pacific in time to bombard the Japanese mainland before the war ended. The ship was decommissioned in 1947. In 1959, a 5-year job began to turn the Chicago into a guided missile ship. The "new" cruiser was recommissioned in 1964, and is still in service.

"Could you find out what the large emblems on the lake end of Navy Pier symbolize? They are huge neon circles each with a 'Y' inside it. They look like peace symbols turned upside down. I've tried everywhere and can't find out what they mean. I believe I've seen the insignia used elsewhere in connection with Chicago."
—Kermit Keough

It took a little tracing. The Chicago Port Authority referred us to the Association of Commerce and Industry, whose predecessor used the symbol in its official seal. We found other evidence, such as the emblem printed here. We finally located the source. The circle with the "Y" is Chicago's emblem. It was chosen as the result of a newspaper contest in 1892. The three sections of the circle represent the three parts of Chicago as divided by river: north, west and south.

"There is a very touching last will and testament on display in one of the courts in the Civic Center. It was written by a lawyer, who at the time was committed to a mental institution. Could you tell me how I can get a copy?"
—Mrs. Leona Rusin

The document is known as the Lounsberry will and you can get a copy by sending a check or money order for $1 to the clerk of the Circuit Court Probate Division, Room 1202, Civic Center, Chicago 60602. The story is that it was found in the ragged coat pocket of an insane old man at Chicago State Hospital. It is a good story and a very beautiful will. The tale, however, is pure fabrication. The legacy was written by poet Wilston Fish. That fact, we believe, doesn't diminish its beauty and so we are printing the first few paragraphs.

A L E G A C Y

I, Charles Lounsberry, being of sound and disposing mind and memory, do hereby make and publish this my last will and testament, in order, as justly as may be, to distribute any interest in the world among succeeding men.

That part of my interests which is known in law and recognized in the sheep-bound volumes as my property, being inconsiderable and of none account, I make no disposition of in this, my will. My right to live, being but a life estate, is not at my disposal, but, these things excepted, all else in the world I now proceed to devise and bequeath.

Item: I give to good fathers and mothers, in trust, for their children, all good little words of praise and encouragement, and all quaint pet names and endearments; and I charge said parents to use them justly, but generously, as the deeds of their children shall require.

"I have been told by a friend that the Chicago police don't have legal ticketing power at O'Hare International Airport because it is outside the city limits. I would like to know if this is true and, if so, how to go about getting charges dropped on a speeding ticket I got there."—J.F.M.

Tell your amateur lawyer friend he is wrong. O'Hare is very much a part of Chicago and was annexed twice. The 1,080-acre site was deeded to the city as airport surplus at the end of World War II. It was not actually annexed to Chicago until 1956, however. The city used a 33-foot strip of Higgins Road to fulfill the requirement of it being "contiguous" with the city. The Illinois Supreme Court questioned similar annexations in 1959 and Chicago traded the Higgins Road strip to Rosemont for a 185-foot strip along Foster Avenue and then reannexed O'Hare. In other words, you have to pay the ticket.

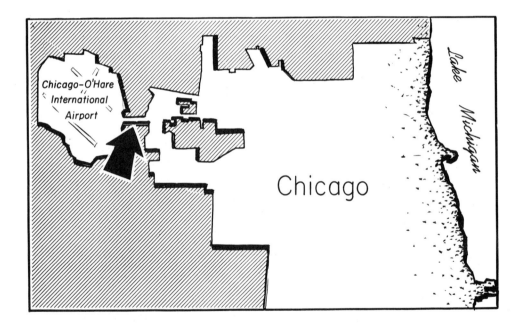

Chicago-O'Hare International Airport

Chicago

Lake Michigan

"Is the beacon on top of the Playboy Building still used for guiding airplanes and ships?"
—Mrs. Ruby Peters

Yes, although it has lost much of the importance it had during the 1930s and 1940s. Commercial airplanes now use radar and all the lakers have it. Ship pilots, however, use several reference points and the Playboy beacon, since it can be seen half way across the lake, is still one of them. Light planes and pleasure craft still rely heavily on the beacon's power.

"Since I am a sentimental person, I have very tender feelings about Chicago's once-fabulous Edgewater Beach hotel. My memories only go back as far as the 1950s, and I wonder if you would be kind enough to print a picture of the famous beachwalk."
—Marion J. Thomas

The Edgewater Beach Hotel, when it rose in all its pink stucco, quasi-Spanish glory in 1916, had more than 1,000 feet of beach promenade on Lake Michigan. Construction of Lake Shore Drive separated it from the lake.

"Can you help a Bohemian mushroom lover? Like my ancestors, I am a dedicated 'houby' (mushroom) hunter, but I've never seen a mushroom farm. Could you find one for me to visit?"—R.S., Berwyn

We found a couple for you. They're listed in the Yellow Pages. The owners aren't too anxious to let you in the actual houses, though, because they believe you could bring a disease into the building and ruin the whole house. They will, however, let you look in the door. Locally, we hope you won't miss the Berwyn-Cicero Houby Festival in early October. The sponsors provide a parade, a "Houby Queen" contest, mushroom-hunting competition and sidewalk displays. If you want to enter either your mushrooms or a girlfriend, contact the Cermak Road Business Association office at 2130 S. 61st Ct., Cicero.

"Would you please tell me in what year the Maxwell Street market began? Also, could you give me a little history behind the market?"
—Susan Neubert

Chicago's open-air flea market is well over 100 years old and probably has suffered reform that many times. The street was named after Dr. Philip Maxwell, the city's first physician, a dashing man weighing 280 pounds. Merchants opened shops there in 1855. Immigrants turned it into the city's pushcart capital long before the turn of the century, as it served the nearby Jewish and Italian Communities. In 1921 the city council declared the area a fire hazard and ordered the ramshackle sidewalk stands demolished. They did it again in 1935, and in 1936 outlawed "pullers," men hired by merchants to drag reluctant customers into their stores. It has recently avoided reform because it is scheduled to be destroyed by urban renewal.

"Is the Picasso capable of instilling hallucinations? The other day I was staring at it in the Civic Center Plaza when I noticed the building facing it on Dearborn seemed to be leaning. Was I seeing things? Did the Picasso cause the building to tip or was it all a result of the construction work when they built the Civic Center?"
—H.R., Bellwood

Don't blame poor Picasso. The 127 North Dearborn Building has been leaning since 1892 when it was built. It was one of the first steel constructed buildings in the Loop and the engineers apparently made a few miscalculations, but just on its south side.

235

"Looking at it from a profile side, I think the Picasso resembles Mayor Daley, especially the nose, lips, and double chin. Could my suggestion be wrong?"
—Gramma Z.

Your idea most assuredly is not wrong. It is the inalienable right of every Chicagoan to assert what the sculpture means or looks like to him or her. Mayor Daley himself said, "The Chicago Picasso . . very naturally develops dialog and difference of opinion." Or, wait a minute, was that said about Mayor Daley?

index

index

index

index